givenomics

How giving creates sustainable success for
companies, customers and communities

Richard Morris

Givenomics

First published in 2012 by

Anoma Press
48 St Vincent Drive, St Albans, Herts, AL1 5SJ, UK

info@anomapress.com
www.anomapress.com

Book layout by Neil Coe

Printed on acid-free paper from managed forests. This book is printed on demand to fulfill orders, so no copies will be remaindered or pulped.

ISBN 978-1-908746-74-0

A CIP catalogue record for this book is available from the British Library.

This book is available online and in all good bookstores.

Dedication

To my wife Connie – I love you 'all the world'.
Your support and encouragement (as always)
is amazing.

To Alexandra and James – thanks for your patience
and just being brilliant.

To Max – woof!

Approved Testimonials

"Often you'll come across a simple idea and say "why didn't I think of that?" Givenomics is such an idea and it has the power to change the way we think and the communities in which we live. Richard Morris' book embraces the latest technology and shows how personal giving can be made easier to enable individuals, beneficiaries and companies to 'win' at the same time. More importantly, it shows that by satisfying our innate desire to belong and contribute, contribution can empower an individual to thrive and reach out for that 'butterfly' of happiness."

Robert Purcell, Chief Executive East Herts YMCA

"Richard's book is in many ways a revelation. He explains the theory and practice of Givenomics in a very clear and thought-provoking voice. An extremely worthwhile read."

Victoria Stapleton, founder of Brora Ltd

"Occasionally strange portmanteau words creep into the language: stagflation, humongous, infomercial... but now we have one that, if it works, will transform how we give money and how businesses can be part of the solution and not part of the problem. "Givenomics", the new book by Richard Morris, entrepreneur and founder of TheGivingMachine, is a must-read for anyone interested in how our society could be a better place: it's a really good read too."

David Fitzpatrick,Chief Executive, Cynnal Cymru – Sustain Wales

Acknowledgements

I always said I'd write a book but wanted to wait until I found something worth writing about – Givenomics is that something.

There are numerous people to say thanks to but here's a selection:

- Ann and Suzanne for the initial encouragement to go ahead with TheGivingMachine

- Jonathan, Craig and Mark for helping to shape an idea into a real company and sticking with it

- Mario for joining the team to make the board and me more effective

- Luisa, Gina, Lisa, Deb, Claire, Emma, Lara and Karen who have helped, or are still helping, to grow TheGivingMachine

- Connie Morris, Robert Purcell, David Fitzpatrick, Jeremy Spencer, Victoria Stapleton and Robert Ashton who reviewed first drafts and ideas, were honest with their feedback and helped shape up the final draft to what you have in your hand.

Table of Contents

Introduction

Businesses have broken our economy and we all have to literally pay for that. Typically they strive to increase shareholder value by constantly seeking to push more stuff to more customers with 'in your face' sales techniques. These models may hit short-term sales targets but they don't build long-term shareholder value and have little or no benefit for the communities we all live and work in. Never has it been more obvious that businesses driven by greed have caused such incredible and long term damage to an entire economic ecosystem.

Businesses have become a major part of the problem. Doing business the same way and expecting different results is the definition of insanity.

New approaches are required that will transform businesses to become part of the solution. Givenomics is an emerging model that unites companies, customers and communities so all can contribute and thrive.

Current Business Models are not Working

Chasing Profitability Alone is not Good Enough Anymore

Economics – a Definition

Looking up the meaning of economics I found the following definition:

Economics: the branch of knowledge concerned with the production, consumption, and transfer of wealth (Oxford Dictionary).

I am not an economist, but it would seem that our economic models and systems have broken in recent years. There is deep dissatisfaction across the globe with the most profitable companies and the most successful business leaders. This situation is destructive. There is a need to identify ways in which economic models can be more constructive, ways in which new models can be a powerful force for contribution for all and not just the few.

Prosperity should be Celebrated

Ideally, profitable companies should be applauded – they create wealth, the money, in the first place. However, we have seen numerous financial meltdowns in recent years along with the almost incredible behaviour of prosperous people – especially in the banking sector. There has been a growing gap between average earners and top earners in many business sectors. For many, this has led to a general mistrust of prosperity on both a personal and business level. Unfortunately, that mistrust has been well-founded in many cases but this attitude is not a healthy one for any economic community.

We need successful people, successful businesses that make profits, but they need to connect back to the very people and the very communities that help them produce that wealth in a way that builds a more sustainable model for everyone. To date, sustainability is primarily concerned with eco-friendly aspects of conducting business. While these are undeniably important, they do not address the economic problems we face.

We need new approaches to unite commerce, customers and communities in ways that enable them all to experience success:

- Prosperous businesses
- Happy customers
- Thriving communities

The Wealth/Happiness Ratio is not what you Would Expect

There's no getting away from the fact that there will always be more prosperous parts of the world than others. There will be more prosperous countries, businesses and people than others. However, increased wealth has not led to increased happiness and wellbeing. Many studies have been carried out on happiness and how it correlates to wealth, both at an individual and on a country or regional level. However, measuring happiness is obviously really difficult. It's subjective and feelings-based, whereas material wealth is specific and measurable. I know that some economists would still argue with the latter, but in the main, you can put a number to a wealth assessment.

The first interesting outcome is that as a country gets more prosperous, it does not correlate with becoming happier. You would think that prosperity would make you happier but in the main, countless studies show that this is not the case. Looking at the UK and USA over a number of years, the average prosperity and material wealth of people has risen sharply. Just think of all the material goods we take for granted – refrigerators, televisions, computers, mobile phones, cars etc. However, the ability to acquire and have them has not made us happier. Indeed it would seem that by several measures, we are significantly unhappier.

For economists this is a puzzle. After all if you were managing a country, you would want that country to be a happy one and it would seem that making it more prosperous is not a guarantee of that.

A Thriving Nation is not Achieved by Economic Models Alone

So what does happiness relate to in this context? Some studies show that it is the gap between rich and poor that affects overall happiness and this has been widening over recent years in the UK and USA. Perhaps it also relates to the gap between average and top earners and that explains the backlash against the top earners that we see. We can see this in the increasing number of executive pay reviews, shareholder revolts and anti-capitalist demonstrations across the globe.

The current economic models have the appearance of benefiting the few and not the many. New models are needed that connect the wealth-generating engines back to the wider community. It would make a massive difference to how the wider community members think about successful businesses. For example: rather than being jealous, envious or suspicious of success, specifically commercial success, we should want to celebrate it as a way to make an even bigger positive difference to the world around us.

On a personal level, giving, and especially gift giving (not reactive giving for fundraising) does make people happier. Therefore, a more giving society should be a happier one. Just think of how it feels when someone lets you out when you are driving and trying to turn across a road. Hasn't that feeling been one of the great outcomes of the 2012 Olympics? The attitude of people coming together to celebrate the contribution of all athletes has been fantastic. It's simple stuff that has a profound effect when you can encourage, measure and reinforce that behaviour on a national or even global scale.

Existing Marketing Models Prey on Dissatisfaction

Feature Based Advertising is Dead

It's funny when you see the old adverts that used to lead on the features/benefits of a particular product or service. Being an engineer at heart, it would seem a sensible approach to trying to sell your products and services to an audience. After all, that is a logical sales technique.

However, when you talk to the best sales people, they know that selling is an emotional experience. The most important way to think about that is to enable your prospects to believe that your product or service will meet an emotional need within them.

For some businesses in commodity products and services, it may be that only price and features are relevant. These companies will find their existing commercial models do not give them the opportunity to tap into an emotional level. It is just more discounts and special offers and sales. These mechanisms are so prevalent that we become increasingly immune to their messages.

Dissatisfaction as a Buying Motivator

Dissatisfaction has proved a great motivator for customers to buy products to improve how they feel. In our house we often talk to our children about an advert and ask them how it made them feel; what do you think the advertiser wants you to do? How are they making you feel that makes you want to buy their product? We are all being manipulated to a greater or lesser degree when exposed to advertising.

Car adverts are great examples here. They are clearly targeted at specific sections of our society in terms of gender, age and social status. There aren't many that focus heavily on features because let's face it – they all have four wheels, a steering wheel, seats, air conditioning, electric windows etc. They need to focus on how having that car will make you feel – it will make you (and perhaps you and your family/partner/friends) feel happier or more successful for example.

Beauty products for men and women are classics on this topic too. No matter how many times I use my branded razor, my abs will never look like the fellow in the advert for that product. Shame really...maybe one day.

A wealth of research and real, hard numbers over many years show that this form of motivator works and works really well. People want to change themselves for the better and the desire to sell products will continue to push advertising this way.

While this technique works, its wider impact is not necessarily that positive. Driving up sales in some cosmetic products, for example, could easily be seen as spreading dissatisfaction among the population about how they look. The pursuit of profit may come at the expense of a growing feeling of unhappiness in how we look naturally without augmentation.

It is Clearly Time to Rethink the Models that We Have

There is a significant body of evidence suggesting that a more giving and altruistic approach to life and business leads to a higher level of happiness, collective performance and impact. The empirical evidence on a personal level is overwhelming on this subject: giving is a great behaviour to adopt for your wellbeing as well as for the wellbeing of others.

By giving, I mean proactive gifting, not just responding to requests for your money. So now we know this, it seems sensible to re-look at our business models and economic models. We need to see how they can be improved to benefit all stakeholders and make the businesses even stronger to have more impact. Translating that evidence from a personal level into business and economic models can now be done and Givenomics is an example of that. This book outlines a proven small-scale concept to get the ball rolling and foster the contribution from others to help shape it into achieving its potential.

Givenomics

Connecting Commerce, Customers and Communities

The Basics of Givenomics

A business, perhaps your business, invites and enables customers and staff to make a difference to the causes of *their choice* in return for doing what you would like them to do (eg. buy your products). Typically, the most popular marketing incentives are discounts or direct rewards. In Givenomics, the reward is making a difference via causes chosen by the customers (and perhaps staff). At the basic level, that is the magic formula and in my experience with TheGivingMachine, there is evidence that this works. In a Givenomic model, all stakeholders involved want the business to be successful but for different reasons.

The crucial thing to impart here is that the customer has to be able to support something that matters to them – not a shortlist of what matters to the business: for example, any school, charity, or community-aided sports club they choose.

I am a trustee of East Herts YMCA in Bishop's Stortford, a charity that supports young people in the area. In a Givenomic model, I can purchase products and services from numerous companies and each purchase enables a small amount of the sale to go to East Herts YMCA. Using Givenomics, you could purchase the same products and services from the same companies. Those same donation amounts would go to the cause chosen by you, whatever it was and wherever it was.

The result is that:

- I feel good because I'm giving for free when buying from participating companies

- The company is happy because I'm contributing to their commercial goals and am more likely to recommend them to others too

- The companies and their employees are happy because they are contributing to the wider community as part of their commercial activity

- East Herts YMCA is pleased because they are receiving additional income they can put to good use.

When you look deeper, this alignment of goals connects a business much more effectively to the world in which they operate. It motivates people in new ways, ways that connect more deeply. This can then translate into more business, more giving and more value for everyone involved. Givenomics is a powerful model based on sound principles and data.

As a practical example, I choose to buy my office stationery from Viking because 3% of the sale price will be donated to my favourite causes. Viking wins my business. I feel great because I've generated free income for my chosen causes. My causes are happy as they see additional income from Viking and can see I've supported them.

For Businesses, it can Begin as a Cost of Sale

Let's assume that as part of a sales and marketing plan, you have various sales channels out there. Each of them will have a cost to bear. In online affiliate marketing for example, you may choose to offer a sales commission to someone else as a percentage of every sale they generate for you – let's say 3%. I have spent the last few years building TheGivingMachine, a not-for-profit social enterprise, using affiliate relationships to develop a Givenomic model.

Our experience suggests that it is the principle of giving that is more important than the actual value. However, acceptable commission values for low margin goods should ideally be no lower than 1% and for high margin goods, no more than 10%. Above this value, customers are likely to question the level of margin being charged that allows this and below 1%, it looks too meagre or mean.

An advantage of this type of marketing is that the costs are relatively fixed. More sales mean more commissions, more commissions mean more giving and therefore more connectivity of a business to customers and their causes. Less business, of course, means the opposite – but the financial exposure is contained.

Enabling Customers to Give to what Matters to Them

The crucial thing here is to enable customers to give to the causes that *they choose*. These causes should be any charitable cause or school. In the UK, schools are still classed as charitable anyway. For companies wanting to do this on their own, it will be hard since managing the distribution of so many small sums of money is not practical.

In TheGivingMachine system for example, customers can support up to four charity/school choices in any percentage split. Although it would be simpler to limit that to one, our experience suggests that it should be at least two.

There are numerous instances where supporting more than one charity or school becomes important. You might have children in two schools, you might want to support a local charity and a national or international one, or even do a combination of all of these things. The key is to be inclusive and not exclusive. There is always a balance however, and when designing TheGivingMachine, we felt that enabling up to four charities/schools was a good compromise and manageable.

The Power of Givenomics – an Example

A Marketing Agency Decision

I have a couple of examples that help show the impact of Givenomics and how it connects commerce, customers and communities together. In this first example, a popular catalogue clothing retailer had outsourced management of their affiliate marketing (sales referral marketing) to an external agency. This agency had done a review of partners working for their client and ranked them in terms of the percentage of repeat business vs. new business.

Sometime in early 2010, TheGivingMachine was informed that it was just under the target for the percentage of new business being referred and that the arrangement was being reviewed and may have to come to an end. I understand that from a pure analytical business point of view. It makes perfect, practical sense. After all, I would imagine that all the other sales partners of this clothing retailer were for-profit organisations and some must have been performing better than TheGivingMachine for bringing in a higher percentage of new customers. We know that there were many other sales partners who also fell short of these thresholds.However, there was one big difference. TheGivingMachine was giving away 75% of the sales commissions generated to schools and charities chosen by customers. I felt that we were positively impacting the brand and suggested that the marketing agency might like to take that into account. The difference between the actual performance and their threshold was very small and I was therefore hopeful. I recall that TheGivingMachine had referred about £400,000 worth of business at that time and had therefore received a fair amount of commission from thousands of purchases – each generating a sales commission and therefore a donation. Each purchase connected a customer, a cause and this retailer in a positive way.

The agency would not be swayed by this argument and notified TheGivingMachine that we had to cease our arrangement with their client going forward. We duly let TheGivingMachine audience know of the change.

The Impact

The effect of communicating this change to TheGivingMachine community was nothing short of amazing. It was clear that customers, and even heads of charities, were contacting this clothing retailer saying that generating donations when they shopped was really important to them. They felt that the decision was not in line with this company's publicised social responsibility statements and could not understand why they were doing this.

Here is a typical example of the many items of correspondence I was copied into:

"I was disappointed to learn that you have decided to withdraw your link with TheGivingMachine. Although, I appreciate, you are a business focussed on profitability, I do think that the giving factor has been a huge credit to you. On a personal level, I would think twice about which set of, for example, curtains or larger products I bought if I knew that for the same price (but with a donation to my selected charity), I could go elsewhere. It would be great if you could reconsider this decision with the holistic approach to customer satisfaction I had thought was core to X's values and is certainly key to your online competitors."

The sheer emotion conveyed in this and the many others gave us the first real demonstration that there was something bigger here than just converting sales commissions into donations. It was touching people and organisations in ways that we had not fully appreciated before.

A Change of Decision

The good news is that shortly after this large flow of communication to this retailer, I received a phone call from them (not their agent) saying that it had been an oversight and that they wanted to connect back to TheGivingMachine. Needless to say, TheGivingMachine reconnected and we still work well with this retailer today.

I saw this as a win on two levels. Firstly, it was a win for the customers and community organisations that convinced a high street retailer that giving to causes chosen by customers is very, very important to them.

I also saw this as a win for the retailer as they restored good will quickly and could see that in addition to a sales commission structure, they were part of a partnership that was helping their brand as well as their bottom line – something that I feel is the best formula for a great partnership and an effective example of why Givenomics has enormous potential.

However, I was too busy working with the rest of TheGivingMachine Team to keep growing the social enterprise to think too much more about this idea at the time.

Givenomics Takes Shape

How Givenomics Benefited Amazon

Early on in 2012, I started considering how I could communicate the concept of giving being good for the business community. I was invited to speak at a social enterprise event in Norwich and share my experience and how it related to this idea. I had always been clear on where we were going and what the goals were long-term, but there's nothing like a speaking opportunity to help you stop, take stock and make time to refine your outlook.

I took some time out of the operational part of the business so that I could review what had been achieved to date and to analyse the statistics and information that would help to develop a more holistic look view of TheGivingMachine's performance in terms of financial and social impact.

I had also been reading about the psychology of giving, where altruistic behaviour ends up being beneficial to the giver as well as the gift receiver. Could understanding what leads to happiness on an individual level help develop a model that could work in a commercial environment?

As I looked at the data, and considered the psychology, I was struck by the idea of how the concept of giving could positively impact a large scale economic model. The word Givenomics came to me then as the perfect description of such a concept.

I saw Givenomics as an extension of the definition of economics to become the branch of knowledge concerned with production, consumption, and transfer of wealth to benefit companies, customers and communities.

As one of TheGivingMachine's more popular shops, I decided to look at the performance of Amazon over 2011 in more detail.

Amazon Performance on TheGivingMachine 2011

Since there are a number of statistics available, I have just focused on the main ones. Namely:

- 130,000 purchasing events made with Amazon via TheGivingMachine worth over £2m in sales

- This generated a corresponding 130,000 donations at no additional cost to the shopper

- The donations were generated by 14,000 different people

- £70,000 in free donations was raised

- Over 3,000 UK schools and charities benefitted

Amazon has many partners referring sales to them via many different websites and so this commission and sales flow is relatively small compared to the overall Amazon UK sales performance. However, the impact and benefit to Amazon, their customers and UK communities goes well beyond just these numbers.

The Impact of Givenomics for Amazon Shoppers

Firstly, let's consider the shoppers. All 14,000 of these people, including me, had joined TheGivingMachine and chosen their favourite causes to support. Every purchase they made, just by choosing to click through TheGivingMachine website and choosing to buy from Amazon, generated a free donation.

A few days later, each of these 14,000 people would have received a confirmation email telling them that their action had generated a donation and telling them that their giving account had been updated. These simple emails are some of the most popular ones we send because people always want to know they have made a difference. Many then go on to click through the link to show them information about their most recent donations.

This information clearly showed Amazon, and any other shops used via TheGivingMachine, as the source of the donations for their chosen causes. When the monthly reconciliation is done and donation payments sent out, these 14,000 people along with everyone else who generated donations via other shops would have received another notification thanking them for their actions and confirming that a payment had been sent to their chosen cause. This again reaffirms that their actions have made a difference.

I felt that this must have a positive impact on how shoppers feel about the shops they are buying from and undertook a survey to test it. I asked whether people registered on TheGivingMachine (givers) felt that their opinion of a shop had been impacted by their participation in the scheme.

Over 85% of those who responded to the survey said that they thought of shops that participated in the Givenomic scheme either "more positively" or "much more positively".

I thought that this was a great initial result that lined up well with what I expected. It also explains why customers were so disappointed when, in the previous example, the clothing retailer left the scheme. The goodwill being generated conflicted with the shop's subsequent behaviour. I am looking forward to undertaking more research on this area in the future.

The Impact for Causes Supported by Amazon Shoppers

There were over 3,000 charities and schools supported by the 14,000 givers. Each of these causes can track where their donations are coming from via TheGivingMachine. Therefore, in amongst the other shop names, Amazon will invariably crop up fairly often. So these beneficiaries know that some of the payments they receive are thanks to both their supporters for choosing to support them, as well as Amazon in sourcing their element of the donations and associated payments.

All this happens automatically and without Amazon having to do anything. It also all happens automatically without the cause having to do anything other than encouraging supporters to join in and make a difference when they shop online.

Does Givenomics Conflict with Affiliate Marketing Objectives?

This is an interesting question. While the initial Givenomic model I have described relies on the established affiliate marketing infrastructure, I expect it to evolve well beyond that in the future. However, I wanted to briefly discuss this aspect as it shows an interesting angle.

Many shops that use affiliate marketing to drive up sales do so with the view that this is just a customer acquisition facility. A shop sets up a commission arrangement for others to direct customers to their website. If a transaction takes place, they pay the commission but they also capture the customer's details and can subsequently market directly to them. They can then hopefully cut out the affiliate sales partner for future transactions involving that customer.

However, using the model as we have discussed, it is clear that I would want to be encouraging people to keep generating these commissions and therefore donations. Perhaps we should look at how the incentives work a bit more closely. For the traditional website that makes money via referrals, the amount of the commission makes a massive difference and if they know that they are really looking to capitalise on the first introduction of a customer to a shop – that makes sense.

In the Givenomic model, it is the long term relationship that is important and so a lower commission level will not necessarily have the same adverse impact compared to traditional affiliate marketing drivers. The giver is motivated to make a difference when they shop, and so a 4% commission is unlikely to affect the behaviour vs. a 3% one for example. It is the combination of repeated behaviour, result, impact and feedback that has the principal value to the main person in this value chain – the shopper.

Therefore, the actual value of commission is not the prime motivator either for TheGivingMachine or, it appears, for the giver. I find this quite astounding really when you think about how the whole affiliate industry is all about statistics and revenue. When you put a giving element right into the middle of it, the drivers and resulting impact change radically – it's almost magic.

TheGivingMachine

A Brief History

TheGivingMachine experience has provided the platform on which to develop the Givenomics concept and so I felt that I should give a more detailed overview of how it came to be, what it does and how it is run. It is unlike any organisation I have been involved with before and all the better for that too.

I was fortunate enough to have been one of a small team that co-founded a company called NorthPoint in San Francisco where we rolled out one of the first national, broadband networks across more than 30 US states. Being one of eight people who started NorthPoint in 1996, leading the engineering and network rollout and helping to grow the company to over 1,000 employees by 2000, was an incredible experience. In early 2000, we returned to the UK and after carrying on for a while in the telecoms and start-up area, I decided to change my career to spend more time contributing back in some way, be more local and be able to spend more time with my wife, young daughter Alexandra and latterly, our son James.

I started getting involved with local voluntary work and while I enjoyed that immensely, I found that I wanted to do something that would contribute more. I'm a 'builder' by nature and so the idea of building a company to help people give money away to their causes in an innovative way really motivated me.

After a conversation with my friend Jonathan Bayly, a business model was identified that could do that and the two of us teamed up with two other local businessmen (Craig McKenzie and Mark Clark) to consider the idea.

Looking at the concept and what we wanted to achieve, we agreed that it should be a not-for-profit company (even though we were all from commercial backgrounds) and we started TheGivingMachine as a local social enterprise in late 2006.

Figure 1: TheGivingMachine Beginnings (Jonathan, Me, Mark and Craig – seated)

I still find it amazing that Jonathan, Mark and Craig have stayed so true to the original vision of what the organisation was set up to do. They are involved in their own businesses and have had many reasons to drop a project that has not covered the cost of their time or yet been able to fully cover the costs of their contribution. Without them, the project and Givenomics would not have the chance to make a difference on such a large scale.

In 2007, the TheGivingMachine service began to spread by word of mouth further afield and then started spreading nationally which was incredibly encouraging.

How TheGivingMachine Works

Every year online shops pay millions of pounds, in fact hundreds of millions, in sales commissions to other websites for referrals. You may search for a product or service on the internet, or maybe visit a comparison website, click on a link and then make a purchase. In many cases, you have just generated a sales commission for someone else. And this goes on every day, every hour, every minute behind the scenes without you realising it. What if you could build a mechanism to generate those sales commissions and convert them into donations to the causes chosen by the shoppers? Well that's what TheGivingMachine does.

For the online shops, they work with many, many sales channels and just pay them a percentage of the purchase for referred business. It is a cost of sale with no risk, as that cost is factored into the price. And the price is no more than if customers buy elsewhere.

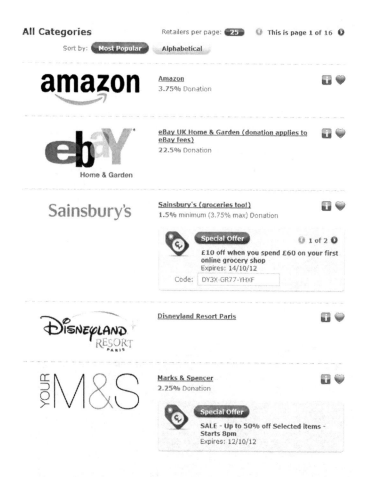

75% of the gross commission revenue becomes a donation and this is the value displayed on the website (see Figure 2). The remaining 25% of the gross commission contributes towards running TheGivingMachine website and distributing the many thousands of donation payments a year.

Each shop sets its own sales commission rate but, to give an example, a shop pays 5% commission for every referred sale, £100 of spend will generate £5 as a commission and £3.75 now becomes a donation for the causes of the buyer's choice.

All the shopper has to do is visit TheGivingMachine website first and choose to buy via one of the 400+ participating shops by clicking through to their website and then buying in the normal way. By clicking via TheGivingMachine website, the shop will track any sales referred by TheGivingMachine with a commission (and therefore donation) being generated.

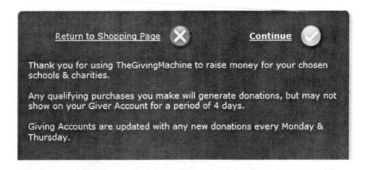

Figure 3: TheGivingMachine click through

Schools and Charities join the scheme as it is easy to promote and generates a steady income. What could be easier than asking supporters to help make a difference at no extra cost?

The hard bit is tracking the many thousands of transactions and handling the many distribution payments every month to causes all over the UK, big and small. All these purchase/donation events are then reported to customers (givers), the causes they support and the shops they buy from.

Why People like this Model

The call to action is really simple for everyone: make a difference to the causes of your choice today at no extra cost to you.

1. Join and choose your cause

2. Shop as normal via TheGivingMachine

3. Give for free with every purchase

It really is as simple as that and, in today's financial climate, the free aspect is really compelling – it becomes a gift rather than a financial donation decision.

Additional feedback we have received is that because any UK charity or school is supported, it really does encourage a more proactive approach to giving. While most people are invited to support a specific school or charity, they are at liberty to change these choices at any time.

When you join as a giver, you can search for your charity or school but if a particular cause hasn't joined yet, you can nominate it and begin supporting it right away. The idea was always to be as inclusive as possible.

How it Works for Charities and Schools

When we set up TheGivingMachine, we decided that we wanted to support credible causes but would not easily be able to define and assess the criteria for 'credible'. So we decided on charitable organisations and schools. All these charities and schools have to do is to complete a simple application form and then one of our team will review that application, check the details and approve it if all is OK. Charities and schools then get access to free downloadable promotional materials to be able to let their supporters know how they can help even more by using TheGivingMachine.

Once donations have been received from the participating shops, they are credited to charity and school accounts on TheGivingMachine. Payments are then sent out monthly for those where relevant thresholds have been reached. These thresholds are set deliberately low (eg. £15) to ensure that donations can be distributed as quickly possible for smaller causes.

Charities and schools can access reports on the donations and payments so that all aspects are as transparent as possible.

How it Works for the Retailers

From a retailer perspective, TheGivingMachine started out as just another sales channel like so many others. TheGivingMachine refers sales to the retailer and gets paid a pre-determined commission for each one. It's a very simple relationship and one that, from a retailer's perspective, is measured by the number of transactions referred and their sales value. These sales commissions can be considered as an ongoing marketing cost.

We receive a number of special offer details which we can use in bulletins and as TheGivingMachine audience has grown, it now attracts exclusive offers too that lend even more credibility to the relationship between retailers and TheGivingMachine.

The really interesting thing is that we have seen a growing number of retailers begin to see that the impact is so much more than just referred sales – it enhances their brand and relationship with customers too. That marketing cost is working much harder for them using this business model and I'll be covering that in more detail later.

What has TheGivingMachine Achieved?

Community Size and Impact

By mid 2012, over 50,000 people had joined TheGivingMachine website to make a difference to the causes of their choice. These members (or 'givers') come from all over the UK and can currently buy from over 400 leading online brands to generate free donations. Around 5,000 different charities and schools are supported with many of the charities being local, community-based organisations. Being free to join, this membership grows daily.

This audience had also generated over 500,000 free donations by just changing their behaviour slightly when shopping online. This is the result of an average growth rate of approximately 40% a year for the last few years.

Each one of these generated donations represents a conscious decision, a proactive choice to make a difference. It was not in response to someone asking for their money. I think that this is amazing and when we see some of the comments back from givers, you can see the passion that they have to make a difference.

The 50,000 people support almost 5,000 different schools and charities across the UK. Many members have been regularly active, some have been sporadically active and a few have never engaged beyond joining.

The Passion is Evident

This passion is not solely about the donation amounts but about the principle of being proactive to make a difference. For example, there are the odd glitches in tracking these sales commissions and if, on the rare occasion, there is a problem, it is brilliant to see that someone cares that a 25p donation is not showing as it should. In a purely commercial world, you might not bother to look into it but that query represents a customer who wants to know that their donation is correctly recorded and sorting that out is incredibly important. The act of generating a donation, of choosing to make a difference is as important as the money.

Here are some of the quotes from TheGivingMachine community:

"I think TheGivingMachine is a fantastic idea."

"Another way of supporting my child's school doing something that I love – shopping!"

"It's very easy to explain TheGivingMachine to our supporters who love the idea of giving us extra money at no extra cost to them."

These examples show that this form of giving while you shop seems to tap into a very powerful human desire to make a difference and can engage people at a far deeper level than other marketing incentives on their own.

The Team that Delivers TheGivingMachine

I want to mention the team that operates and delivers TheGivingMachine service because it is very different in structure from any commercial venture I have been involved with. The same, if not more, passion is there to help the growing community have a massive and positive impact initially in the UK but, in time, well beyond it too.

Being a not-for-profit social enterprise and redirecting 75% of the commission income as donations means that operational budgets were incredibly tight in the early days and so there were no premises. The technical resources were subcontracted to a creative design agency owned by Craig, one of the four founders I mentioned earlier. The operational team handling the day-to-day items consists of five mums (Luisa, Gina, Deb, Claire and Lisa) who work around school drop off and pick up times in a combination of home-based working, kitchen tables, as well as more formal office space during the working week.

I use the term 'mums' in a purely admiring way. I was once chided over this reference by someone in a commercial company we met with, but that is what they call themselves with pride. TheGivingMachine demographic audience has so far tended to be women between the ages of 25 and 44 – typically mums. Since so many of the initial causes to join TheGivingMachine were schools, it made sense to recruit our team to understand this market and the Parent Teacher Associations (PTAs) that help them. Typically therefore, most of the operational team have been mums over the last few years.

Using various technology options out there, you can build and run a flexible and distributed organisation this way as long as you have a great team of people who want to make it happen. When I was helping to roll out one of the first broadband infrastructure networks, we all saw it as a revolution that would provide a level playing field enabling more businesses to compete locally and globally. It's great to be part of that revolution now.

The Value of Networks is in their Connectivity

What is Network Value?

Network Value – the Basics

When I was an undergraduate at the University of York studying electronic engineering, I remember covering this area in great depth. Don't worry, I'm not going all mathematical but there are some aspects of this that are directly relevant to the subject of Givenomics as it relates to connecting businesses, customers and staff in new ways.

The relationship we covered related to Metcalfe's Law, which in essence states that a network's value is related to the square number of endpoints in it. This law was proposed for the first Ethernet data networks where endpoints were devices that communicated with each other in a network.

In the diagrams opposite, you can see that the number of connections goes up exponentially:

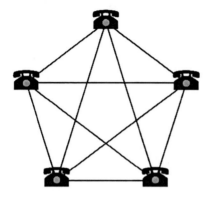

$$\frac{n(n-1)}{2}$$

The relationship is which to boil it down means that the value of a large network grows in proportion to the square of the number of nodes (n^2).

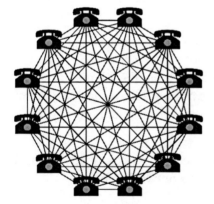

Figure 4: Network Connections (source – wikipedia.org)

To give you an idea of what that means see the chart below:

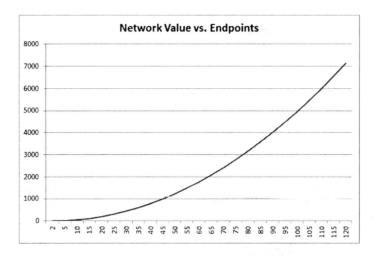

Figure 5: Network Value vs. Endpoints

If we think of a network of mobile phones or email addresses, two people can only talk to each other but 100 people have 4,950 different combinations of point to point communications.

Network value therefore becomes exponentially much more valuable the larger the network gets.

Network Value Limitations and Extensions

There are of course significant drawbacks with any model but the important thing is to understand the underlying principles that give you an approximation or an understanding of a phenomenon. Network value is significant in our internet world because we are all connected to each other in so many ways. If you wanted to get in touch with me (I'd love to hear from you by the way), you can connect to me via phone, email, a multitude of social networks or by post. Suddenly you start to see that the overall network has massive value and therefore networks within networks can have significant value too.

I would suggest that there are a couple of other attributes that are worth considering when we apply this thinking to real people and messages that are communicated within the network.

1. Engagement of message/communication

2. Frequency of message

We all get lots of messages/communications every day. It is a constant battle for senders to get our attention and for us to decide which ones we will give our attention to. Therefore, the value of a network as it pertains to a particular topic or theme is going to vary based on how much it engages us or perhaps how much it inspires us to do something.

The second attribute relates to our attention span. We could get a very relevant message but only once a year and so the value of that connection is less than receiving a very relevant message much more frequently. Of course, messages that become too frequent start to impact engagement and so there is a link between them and they are not independent of each other.

For example, friendships and their value to both people are often characterised by connecting up in some way quite frequently and chatting over whatever has been going on in each other's lives since the last time you met up.

It's simple stuff but it relates directly to how to make networks more valuable to the people within them.

How Network Value Applies to an Organisation

So how does this relate to an organisation? All organisations have a network of customers, suppliers and staff. The old style of communicating will be via the broadcast method, the one-to-many for example. This could be via internal memos from the management team or as broadcast marketing to customers. Today, however, all these people can connect to each other in ways that they control, such as social media groups, and can therefore impact your organisation in a huge variety of ways.

Looking at the previous section, there are some implications that are very relevant

1. You want to make sure that you are connected to those networks to be able to see and participate in conversations that are either about, or impact, your organisation in some way

2. You want to ensure that your communications engage people in what matters to them

3. You want to ensure that your communications have the right frequency to maximise the engagement.

In this way, you can leverage the maximum value of networks for your organisation.

An Example

A Retailing Organisation

Let's consider an example of an organisation that sells products or services to customers. It has 50,000 customers on its database. I know that there are many, many attributes that we could then go into, but I'm going to keep it basic to illustrate the point.

Although these customers are interconnected via the various networks we have such as phone, internet, postal etc., they are not really interconnected because they don't actually have any notion that each other exists. They could contact each other and share information but we know that almost all of them won't.

Therefore, at the simplest level, we have a one-to-many network with 50,000 separate communication paths.

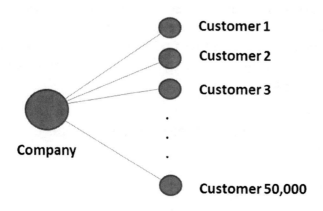

Figure 6: One-to-many Network

The Potential vs. Actual Value

As we have seen above, if everyone was connected in some way to this company with engaging communication flow at the right frequency, the maximum value would be over 1.2 billion. That's a massive difference. Just think about how that could translate into more business, more advocacy for an organisation, more goodwill towards a brand.

In reality, it will be somewhere in between as there are already some customers and staff discussing the organisation via various social networks, rating and commenting on their products and services on other websites.

For the example above, I would bet that the actual value will be much closer to the 50,000 mark, for almost all similar companies, than it will be to the 1.2 billion mark.

I'm also sure that you would have thought, 'yes, but in addition only a percentage of those 50,000 customers engaged in any communication or interaction with that company'. Of course that's true too, but I hope that the basic philosophy of engagement and network value makes sense.

Network Value Dramatically Increases with Givenomics

A Revised Example

If we continue with the example of the company with 50,000 customers – let's suppose that they have implemented some form of Givenomic aspects into their company. They engaged customers by helping to support the causes that mattered to them with every purchase.

This has a number of really important impacts to the network value:

- The engagement between the company and their customers is no longer just about product or service need, it also includes making a difference, an impact to their community and beyond. It becomes more emotional, more meaningful and takes some pressure off the product or service to do all the work for your company success.

- The customer is now also part of a communication event between them and their cause as well as them and the company. They are making a difference because of their choice to buy from that company.

- The customer has now facilitated a communication path between the company and the cause that they chose. The causes should know that they are being supported by this customer as well as the company they have bought from.

Network Values with Givenomics

If all 50,000 customers were included in this new approach, it would treble the communication links possible. If a customer chooses two causes to support, then it multiplies that value by six.

If customers start seeing each other's contributions in joint messaging areas and subsequently share that information, it will add another multiplier into the mix.

By implementing a Givenomic approach, a massive change in network value has been achieved. I'm using network value as a basic metric but the potential to grow and leverage that network is phenomenal. It engages people at a more emotional and impactful level, so it becomes more relevant. As it is connected to their buying behaviour, the frequency becomes something that customers can affect directly with their choices.

It makes the example business a better business in the eyes of all its stakeholders. Its success is meeting commercial and social goals at the same time.

The Givenomic Network Value for Amazon

We've looked at the Amazon performance number earlier. Now let's look at the number of connections that have been made. In the very basic case, there were of course 14,000 connections because there were 14,000 different people buying from Amazon.

If we consider the beneficiaries, we now have at least another 14,000 connections because each giver is connected to at least one cause. In TheGivingMachine system, givers can support up to four causes in any percentage split so let's assume a conservative 10% choose to support two and 10% choose to support three. You then have a maximum of 18,200 causes touched by these 14,000 givers.

There is also a connection between the causes themselves and Amazon, as the tracking reports show where the donations are coming from. Each cause has a representative and so even if they do not share the information with anyone else, there is one person who is part of that connection.

Therefore the total is the sum of:

- 14,000 Amazon – giver connections
- 18,200 giver – cause connections
- 18,200 Amazon – cause connections
- Total = 50,400 a multiple of 3.6!

What was a transactional behaviour has now become a giving behaviour, with a greater likelihood of sharing this information with friends, family, work colleagues etc. either via social networks or just plain old fashioned talking to one another. Therefore, there will also be an uplift in the value. Really conservatively, that might be 10% and that takes it up to over 55,000 and a multiple of about four.

I realise that this is not rigorous mathematics or a recognised formula, but I'm using it to demonstrate the power of this type of connectivity in connecting people, businesses and communities with what seems to be a relatively simple factor, but one that has significant potential to connect commercial success with positive social impact.

The Opportunity is Massive

Customers will Help Businesses Increase their Network Value

By enabling customers and staff to help the causes of their choice as part of a business model, they will be increasing the overall network value. They will be building these connections and the great thing is that with the technology and connectivity available today, it's easier than ever to enable this to happen.

Using the network value approach shows how TheGivingMachine has affected the connectivity between Amazon and the customers that came via TheGivingMachine. In 2011, over 14,000 people made purchases with Amazon via TheGivingMachine. So there were 14,000 connections, if you like, that are just like 14,000 connections Amazon might have had with any of its customers that year. However, those 14,000 people chose over 3,000 different schools and charities to support. Therefore you have a network that connects these three together now in a far more inter-related and meaningful arrangement.

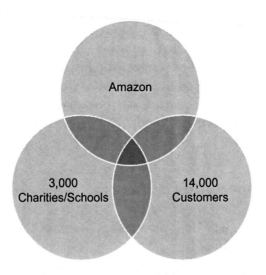

Figure 7: Connecting Amazon, Customers, Charities and Schools

Over 130,000 Amazon purchases were made that year by these customers via TheGivingMachine; just under 10 each, on average. That means the frequency of this connectivity was quite high – something that we already know is important in maintaining a meaningful relationship within a network.

These relationship connections are highly relevant, personalised to each customer, as each purchase directly and positively impacts the causes chosen by the buyer.

The Amazon Lesson for Other Brands

Consider for a moment how those 14,000 customers in the previous section think about Amazon now. In addition to providing a great buying portal, they know that Amazon is helping their causes.

The causes themselves know where the money is coming from and so there is positive reinforcement of the Amazon brand to the 3,000 schools and charities which have financially benefited from this arrangement.

You can see that these numbers and their impact become very relevant in a competitive world. It puts the customers where they want to be. Customers are empowered to make a difference and their positive feelings towards the organisations that help them do that have a significant impact on their perception and attitude towards those brands.

Increasing the Opportunity

There are ample opportunities to increase the impact of a Givenomic approach further. People are more likely to share news that relates to how their choices are positively impacting the world around them rather than just purchasing information. Therefore, social media connectivity to the purchasing events has the potential to increase the opportunity for commercial success and social impact at the same time.

I haven't yet touched on how the causes themselves can be active agents here. When the causes can see how well the commercial sector is helping them via the customer base, there are opportunities for personal stories and other public relations activities. The great thing is that they will not have been manufactured in an office somewhere, they will be as a direct result of real people making real choices and so have more credibility.

There are many, many more areas that could increase the opportunity of Givenomics to benefit a business and that could take up more chapters, but the intention of this book is to get the concept out there and connect with other people who are asking the same questions:

- How can commerce, customers and communities thrive together?

- What economic models do we need right now?

- Which businesses want to be part of the solution?

- What can we do as individuals to change the future for the better?

It's a Tough Climate Out There

The Challenge for Businesses

Customers Have Less to Spend

It's the middle of 2012 as I am writing this and the latest retail news is that Clinton Cards has gone into administration and has now been acquired by American Greetings. It's another potential change to the high street where I live in Bishop's Stortford. There are now a large number of 'to let' signs where H. Samuel the jeweller and Pizza Hut – as well as many independents – used to be.

It's no surprise that much of this change is driven by the fact that customers have less money to spend and therefore either cut back on some items completely or try to reduce costs by buying the items they want more cheaply. Whatever the cause, spending patterns have changed and are changing significantly. Looking at the trend going forward, it is unlikely that many customers will have additional spending power very soon as the costs of living are not likely to reduce and people's incomes are not likely to significantly increase in the near term. It's a tough climate in which to run and grow a business and although there are many business failures, there are many successes too – they just don't make the news.

Brand Differentiation is Becoming Harder

Previously companies could rely on product differentiation and the relevant features, functions, capabilities to help sell products and services. And while this may still be the case if you are first to market, the global marketplace and communication capabilities will ensure that when a good product or service arises, it will get copied quickly. Those features that you were so proud of have become 'old hat'.

Companies rely more and more on brands as they grow. We only have to look at car advertising, for example, to see how the targeting is all about what kind of customer you are and are you right for that type of vehicle. Are you a family person or are you single and want to have loads of friends? This brand aspect is becoming more important in the noisy world we live in. If you are a business owner, how does your company stand out from the crowd?

The rise of online shopping and shopping aggregators like Amazon, Google, Compare The Market and others, re-selling or referring products and services to customers, has made it easy to find the lowest prices. Price sensitivity in customer buying behaviour is squeezing companies out of the middle ground. You are either tending towards the high quality, high margin side of things or the volume, low margin side of things. Being in the middle means that you are likely to be taken out by competition from above and below. For many companies, it is a volume game unless you have a niche, high quality product or experience.

The Online Buying Trend Commoditises Price

Online buying is clearly here to stay and will continue to grow as more and more people take to it. It is no longer a new thing to do, it is just part of our lives. The convenience and cost savings are just too good to pass up. Even though I'm in an online business myself, my wife Connie is still passionate about buying from local shops where we can. I think we have a great balance but the overall trend makes it tougher and tougher for those businesses which rely on bricks and mortar premises. The overheads are so much higher than a cost-effective warehouse with staff and a transaction website.

I've already mentioned the impact that Amazon, Google, Compare The Market and others have on the brand positioning, but the price commoditisation means that margins are being squeezed just to stay in business. With so many other businesses able to access the market of customers, the trend is to enable companies to effectively buy market share with the lowest price and that will obviously favour those with the lowest cost base. Needless to say, that will affect companies that are too slow to spot that trend, re-look at their business and see how it relates to their customers and the marketplace in general.

The Effects of these Trends are Accelerating

The trends of price commoditisation, customer spending capability and price sensitivity are all creating a perfect storm which will unfortunately result in more business failures. We are likely to see more familiar companies failing over the next few years than we have seen for a long time. Having been in business for 50 or 100 years is a great credibility statement that no longer guarantees that a company will be around tomorrow. The changes are too drastic, the competition too high, the customer behaviour changes too different.

In the short term, none of the contributing factors look like they will change their impact and if anything, it looks like they will accelerate their effect. Price will be the main driver unless there is a strong brand differentiator to persuade a customer that there is a reason to make another choice. And even then, for many it would have to be a small change in price rather than a step change.

Businesses Need to Change to Succeed

There are plenty of other books and great people out there who focus on specific markets and types of business but let's agree that, as the old adage goes, 'doing the same thing and expecting different results is stupidity'. It's a favourite saying in my house when I'm in parent mode.

However, I think that the area which offers the greatest opportunity is how to impact the way customers relate to a brand. How can a business become more important to customers in addition to meeting product feature and price requirements? Leveraging new ways to engage with the marketplace can provide a great opportunity to re-establish their brand, to reduce price sensitivity, and connect at a deeper level with their audience, and thus induce higher loyalty and engender increased brand advocacy.

Yes, it is a tough climate out there but for those that can see and work with the trends, it is also a great opportunity. Not all companies are able to think like that. It is not a half full/half empty approach, it is the approach of someone who wants to win in a tough game.

Customers are Finding it Tough Too

There is Far Less Money to Spend

In the previous section, I've considered the business point of view and touched on the customer point of view but I feel that we should look at this in greater detail to better understand the people businesses rely on to buy their products and services – in many cases, people just like you and me.

Our cost of living has dramatically changed over the last few years. We just need to look at fuel costs and the impact of that when we have had colder winters and summers than usual here in the UK. Most people I have talked to have turned the thermostats down a degree or two in their homes. I remember a few years ago that one of my work colleagues said that he had disconnected his main house thermostat from their heating system. He had connected a secret thermostat so he could keep energy costs down but let others in the house think they could change it. That's a bit drastic but clearly the drive to save money is strong!

Since the market crash a few years ago, credit is harder to obtain for many people. The result is that many are saving the deposits they need for mortgages while currently renting or still living at home. The number of home purchases has fallen dramatically and even government incentives for first time buyers have not made a massive and sustained difference.

The word 'austerity' is on the media pages every day and so, even if many people could afford to buy some extras, some luxuries, there is a cautious mood. Combined with uncertainty, this obviously affects buying behaviour.

A Climate of Frugality and Deals

The current situation for customers has helped encourage the rapid rise of a number of companies specialising in discounts and coupons, which gives short term relief to businesses in terms of bringing in revenue and, hopefully, repeat customers. However, the customer acquisition cost for businesses is high and many businesses have found it hard to fulfil the rapid rise in orders at such low prices.

The other impact of these types of companies and indeed, the continued discounting by shops to attract business, is that no one really expects to pay the recommended retail price (RRP) any more. There are regular stories in the media about retailers showing discounts from RRP where RRP has been fiddled in some way. No one wants to pay full price for anything and retailers have helped promote this attitude and concept to win in the short term.

A Suspicion of the Commercial System

The crash of the banking system is still affecting the global financial sector well after the event. It has had the effect of creating a general mood of suspicion that the 'system' is out for itself and benefits at the expense (literally) of everyday consumers. This suspicion has been transferred to everyday commercial businesses, not just banks. It helps explain why there is a greatly increased interest in social enterprise models.

The real powerhouses are normal commercial companies, with profitability being a fair measure of business success. The challenge is that this climate of suspicion and judgment means customers want companies to be successful so that they are still around tomorrow, but not so successful that they feel robbed. Customers are looking for evidence that companies care about more than just profit.

Only today as I write this, there is yet another story in the business news about a chief executive's pay package being voted down by shareholders. These shareholders have decided that something is not right, although they want success for the company too. So clearly, shareholders are not only starting to feel this issue, but acknowledge that they need to do something about it.

Feelings obviously run very high on this subject, as past riots in London and protests around the world at the capitalist system have clearly demonstrated. I am sure that this has been and will continue to be a hot topic for a long time to come. The banking sector and, to some degree, much of the commercial sector, have lost the trust and support of the very people they rely on to be profitable.

This attitude is therefore a very significant barrier to any commercial business that wants to be successful and to have support from its customers, shareholders and all stakeholders to help generate and sustain success.

There is an Incredible Desire to Make a Difference

The good news is that it's not all doom and gloom. I only have to look around from a slightly different perspective to see the incredible desire that these same people have to make a positive difference in their communities, their country and beyond.

Red Nose Day in 2011 inspired over 750,000 people to phone in on the night. With those individual donations and the many other performances, radio shows and UK-wide fundraising activities, over £74 million was raised. I mention this as an example of how so many people can be inspired to want to make a difference by just one event, on one evening on one day of the year, every two years.

Charlie Simpson, aged seven, raised over £210,000 (£145,000 in the first 48 hours) via his JustGiving page for the 2010 Haiti earthquake relief programme by UNICEF.

Just look at the thousands and thousands of charities (not just the big ones you have heard of) and school Parent Teacher Associations (PTAs) that all rely on the support of people like you and me in large and small groups: the untold masses of people who contribute to their communities with their time, money or both. Despite detrimental changes in financial circumstances, people are still working in so many ways to make their communities better in some way. This is clearly a very powerful motivator for people and linking businesses to it will help rebuild that trust relationship to make it better than ever.

Charities are Finding it Tough

Why Talk about Charities and Schools?

Charities and schools are not just separate entities; they are connected to the communities we live and work in. The people who work with them, govern them and support them are often the same people in commercial businesses.

For a number of years, I have been a trustee and, more recently, Vice Chair of East Herts YMCA in Bishop's Stortford. Like many local charities, it has a direct impact on the community my family and I live and work in, the community where our children go to school, the community we choose to spend recreation time in. Therefore, the welfare of this community is of great importance to me and will affect how I look outside and view the world in general. It will affect my propensity to spend and give and that's why it is important to consider.

Traditional Funding Streams are being Reduced

In my trustee role, I have already seen first-hand, the effect of cuts on some of the funding from the local council. This has often been in the form of renewing contracts to provide services with a 10% or more reduction across the board. Therefore, the charity has reviewed how and where elements of service provision can be revised to still provide a base level service that meets needs. In some cases, long standing contracts have not been renewed or just cancelled to save money.

This story is replicated across the charity sector with a number of programmes being cut or reduced. The impact that this will have is really hard to effectively measure as the outcomes are often very soft and not easily quantified. In some cases these changes will lead to better, more focused and cost effective services but in some, it will leave quite a negative legacy on our communities.

The challenge for many charities, especially those that have grown up as suppliers to local authorities, is to develop new funding streams. To be fair, many have relied too much on this source of funding for too long. As any company knows, if you have a customer who represents a large percentage of income on its own, there's a big risk sitting there. At East Herts YMCA, we are currently in the process of redefining the financial strategy to move to a much more diversified income stream for these very reasons. From conversations I have had with other chief executives and board members, many large and small organisations are doing the same.

Centralisation of Funding is Causing Large Changes

Apart from reducing the amount of money available via local authorities, there is also a significant move to centralise the spend. This clearly makes sense from a commercial point of view but is quite difficult for charities to quickly respond to. Many charities have grown up to match the funding structures and it is not as easy to merge or acquire charities in the same way as commercial businesses can.

East Herts YMCA is in the process of establishing a social enterprise company in partnership with Central Herts YMCA and Watford YMCA to combine forces and meet these centralised tendering requirements. The formation of YMCA Hertfordshire is a truly innovative step and represents a new model for evolving with the times and the needs of the day. It will enable the three charities to bid for county-wide contracts and then deliver the services to their particular regions.

The Need is Getting Larger

I've only really talked about the 'supply' side of the charity chain so far in terms of reduced money available, but if you consider the 'demand' side, in many cases, it is getting larger. There are more homeless people who need help, there are more people in financial difficulty who need help, there are more elderly people who need help in one way or another in their later years, and so it goes on.

From my trustee role with East Herts YMCA, I believe with more income we could help more young people to overcome problems to belong, contribute and thrive in our community. This would clearly help individuals be happier but on an outcome level, become an asset to their community rather than a statistic that numerically shows up as a cost in areas such as benefits, policing etc.

So while the situation is difficult, with my business hat on, there is a rising demand across the board for many targeted services that would positively impact our communities in so many ways.

If we look beyond our own communities, the news is the same from environmental changes to global poverty, hunger, conservation, sanitation and many, many more.

The Key for Charities is to Diversify Funding

By diversify funding, I really mean grow additional funding streams. As I already mentioned, East Herts YMCA is going through this review at the moment and decided that no particular funding stream should be more than 20% of turnover. We thought that this was a good starting point for planning. It would be difficult, but not catastrophic, to lose 20% of turnover. It wouldn't close the charity, for example.

Personally, I was really pleased to see this approach adopted. Being able to operate in a more business-like fashion as a charity board makes far more sense and enables East Herts YMCA to blend ethical and business skills for a more effective organisation.

However, the key issue will always be where is the new money coming from? We have already seen that you can't just rely on direct donations as there is only a finite amount of money out there and, for quite some time, it is unlikely to change significantly to enable people to give more. Always asking for more can alienate many supporters.

Schools are Finding it Tough Too

Increased Costs

Like any other organisations, the increasing cost of energy and supplies hits schools too. The technology needs for many keep rising, as does the cost of maintaining that technology with the right staff. For many schools, especially the larger ones, a full time bursar or financial manager is a must while the smaller ones struggle along with either volunteer support or the staff adding this aspect to their teaching duties. I come into contact with many schools via my role with TheGivingMachine and there is a desperate need for schools to increase their funding to support the educational experience that they give to their pupils.

Like the previous section on charities, I mention schools because even if you don't have children in school right now, you will have customers, staff, shareholders and other stakeholders in your business who do. If you do have children, you will know how important their education is and how strongly you feel about it. People's feelings of support towards schools run very high. And schools struggle, like every other community organisation, to do more with less.

Demand on Schools Continues to Diversify

From the conversations I've had with teachers and parents, the demand, or requirement, to enable pupils to learn the elements from a prescribed menu has become harder than it used to be. It gets harder because the children we send to school have a significant range of differing issues to deal with in order to be able to learn in their school environment.

These issues can be in so many different areas – from behaviour to language development, learning abilities to medical issues and parental support, to just name a few. I mention these issues because they place a heavy burden on our schools that has a cost impact and these costs cannot be met by the state alone. This leaves little additional money for some of the more fun and playful aspects of school, such as funding trips or play equipment that can also have a beneficial impact on a child's personal development.

That's Where Parent Teacher Associations Come in

Parent Teacher Associations (PTAs) for many schools are a crucial part of the overall team. Typically, they co-ordinate fundraising and event management and take much of the pressure for these aspects off the teaching staff. The money they raise on a yearly basis is crucial to funding many of the non-essential items for schools. This could be playground equipment, but increasingly, infrastructure project funding also requires a contribution from the school and PTAs will often take that responsibility to raise a percentage of an overall project.

Having worked with many PTAs across the UK, I think it is amazing to see the support, passion and commitment that people put in to support their schools in this way. In my current team on TheGivingMachine, five of them are currently serving or have served as PTA members in four different schools in the Bishop's Stortford area.

But Parents are 'Maxed Out'

Since parents are normal people like everyone else (not that I always feel that way about myself), the same constraints come into play. The various fundraising techniques used by PTAs for their schools can become too much. After all, there is only so much 'spare' money in everyone's pockets.

Schools often use sponsorship or raffle tickets to raise money but the funny thing is that when we trialled using an online version to do this, it wasn't that successful. It's not surprising when you look in more detail at how these fundraising mechanisms really work. The theory is that parents will be able to ask friends and family to join in and everyone contributes. The reality is that most parents don't feel comfortable asking others to do this and so they complete the sponsorship form themselves and often buy all the raffle tickets as well – who wants to send a full book back to the school and say their friends and relatives don't want to support the school?

Continuing to ask for more money will just become an annoyance and not foster a genuine partnership between school and parents – it is the same issues that charities face with their supporters.

Local Businesses Support Schools, Don't They?

Estate agents have been a mainstay of sponsoring events via signage for summer fairs and bonfire parties etc. Many schools have raffles every year and approach the local community shops to support them by donating great prizes. Talking to PTAs over the last few years, it has become harder and harder for shops to help out as they are feeling the financial squeeze. They have to concentrate on their businesses and, perhaps for many, just staying afloat.

So we'll see many school raffles with prizes that are perhaps not as large as they were, or at least with larger cash prizes coming out of the actual revenue of the raffle itself, so that the end fundraising result is reduced from previous events.

Schools Need to Diversify Sources of Funding and Support

So, like charities, schools need to control costs and at the same time identify new ways to attract funding – preferably in a sustainable, recurring way that does not leave supporters feeling annoyed or cajoled into the activity. Many schools and PTAs will be solving these issues in their own areas in different ways and it will be important to share experiences and achievements between schools to enable everyone to benefit from pioneers in this area. There is also the opportunity to look at these issues together with the business elements discussed earlier, to see how they could be connected in a constructive way for everyone.

A New Way to Look at the Problem

The Connectedness of Business and Community Issues

So, we've looked at the issues that businesses face in terms of brand image, customer retention and differentiation, and we've also reviewed the fact that our communities and people within them are facing significant hardships which mean that consumers will look only for the best deals and will forgo luxuries, which then feeds back into the business issues.

I remember seeing one of my children's books that highlighted how money flows through a community and the cyclical nature of it. The flow has been interrupted by sudden changes in the welfare of some of the key players in the long chain involved and this affects us all. Even if your community and you personally have not been as affected, others who have, such as staff, customers, suppliers, shareholders and so on, are part of wider communities and so these issues are very relevant to them and their families.

Necessity Inspires Change

Tackling these issues well will help build trust between the 'commercial' system and its consumer base and help to meet the need to remain profitable. So, there is a great opportunity here to connect customers, commerce and community organisations in new ways that can create value for everyone and to connect them in ways that build trust, and help all to prosper and thrive.

TheGivingMachine is one of those organisations doing just that and is benefitting from the collective desire to do things differently. The old phrase 'necessity is the mother of invention' comes into play and in this arena there are many organisations working hard to make positive changes in other ways too.

Some Changes are Making People Happier

You would think that having less money would always make people unhappier. In some cases that will be true but there have been reports of some interesting changes in attitudes and behaviour that are having positive impacts on families.

I am sure you have heard of 'staycations'. This is where you would have gone abroad but instead, you do more in your own country or even stay at home and have days out to save the cost of the holiday you might have had previously. In various magazines and papers, there are letters where those on staycations have actually really enjoyed them and not only rediscovered local attractions, but also spent more enjoyable time just being together with other family members.

The same can be seen in the habit of eating out. More people are eating at home and rediscovering a family meal together. While this might initially have been due to family austerity measures, it brings some other benefits too. I'm not saying that this is happening everywhere but where it is happening, it is affecting how people feel.

Volunteering is also on the rise. People are more willing to give their time for free to help community organisations to make a difference. How great is that – during a time of cutbacks, there are still many, many people working hard to help others for no apparent personal gain.

Behaviour changes and re-connecting to family, friends, community organisations and local places are having a positive impact on people's lives.

Understanding community-related drivers and motivations of the very people companies need to support and buy their products becomes increasingly important. Just having a product to sell at a price will not engage people at a deeper level. Creating a positive impact in these areas, and being profitable at the same time, is what Givenomics achieves.

The Rise of Personal Empowerment

Ordinary People Generate Extraordinary Information

The First Internet was about Consumption

In the late 1990s, I found myself leading the network design and testing followed by the initial mass rollout of the broadband internet infrastructure across the USA. The amazing thing was that very quickly there was so much content you could access that made things so much easier in terms of finding information, buying goods and services. Finding opening times for shops, company contact details, train times and so much other basic information became much faster and easier.

One of the conversation topics in offices and homes was all about new website addresses that were either useful, cool or even strange. It was a new frontier where we became consumers of information and those few who knew how to originate information were at the forefront of this frontier.

The growth of both websites and those who accessed this information was exponential and amazing. It opened up a new world – an online world that provided new possibilities for everyone who could connect to it.

The Second Internet Evolved to be about Personal Contribution

This incredibly fast growing network of interconnected devices soon found ways to change the dynamic of how it worked. It began to evolve so that everyday people could actually be sources of information. I'm not talking about those few who could construct their own websites, I'm referring to the widespread use of blog sites and, latterly, social media networks, where people like you and me can join and then share a piece of news, an article, a thought, a photo, a movie clip.

In an instant, we become a source of information that is open to public view. Depending on how it is received, it can become popular overnight ('trend') and rapidly gain followers. Your contribution can become a worldwide hit almost instantly. This interconnectivity and the power that we all have is incredible. We are no longer mainly just consumers of information sourced by a few. We are part of a 'many-to-many' environment that has a significant impact on numerous areas of our lives and our businesses.

The Balance of Information Control has Shifted

In a 'many-to-many' environment, the control of information is no longer centralised in the same way. There will always be aggregators of this information but they have lost their power, their control on information. They became facilitators, not sources.

As an example, you can think of news networks. In the past we would all receive news at the same time via the evening broadcasts or in the morning papers. The information was controlled by these organisations. However, although news organisations still have a major role to play in aggregating this news for us to read, it is now often members of the public who source it. If the news is relevant to you or your area, you will often find out first via another channel of information that could be social media, text, or an email from someone you know or are connected to.

The sources of information that you have access to and the speed with which you can share something important or relevant from your phone is almost instantaneous.

Personal Empowerment Affects a Business

So how does this affect a business? Well, businesses can no longer control the information out there about their business, their products and services and to compete, they may not be able to control how people buy them. Customer needs and wants may define how they sell to their markets.

Of course businesses can influence what people think via marketing but as we all have access to so much data and other people's opinions, marketing goes into a melting pot to be analysed with other information. If a company's outbound communication does not match the reality that others are experiencing, unhappy customers can let the world know about it. If customers love what a company is doing, they will share that too and help grow the business.

Customer service and reputation has become almost as important as the product itself for many successful companies.

Ordinary People Become Agents of Change

This empowerment also means that customers can instigate changes in businesses because they can communicate with each other as well as with your organisation. Earlier, I described how we had a shop leave TheGivingMachine. Their third party marketing agents called me up and said that we were missing a new customer acquisition target by 1% and that it was a policy decision that they would have to stop working with us. I used our statistics and said that we were doing far more than their other partners in building a positive image of their brand and associating them with helping hundreds of schools and charities across the UK.

Despite these strong arguments, they wanted to proceed with leaving our community. It didn't take long for their customers to be calling them and asking why they were leaving a programme that linked this shop with helping their communities. Their customers shared the information with other customers and I know that this company must have received many, many calls and emails.

As you know, a few days later we received a call from this shop who had realised how we were aligned to their social responsibility goals and they have been happily trading via TheGivingMachine website since. This example clearly illustrates that the 'many-to-many' relationships directly affect a business. Staff and customers can become originators of news and of information that can be rapidly picked up and shared to instigate change.

Personalisation is Here to Stay

Supermarket Loyalty Set the Trend

We are now experiencing unprecedented levels of personalisation. Amongst the pioneers of mass personalisation were the supermarkets with their loyalty schemes. By capturing very detailed information about us and our buying habits, targeted advertising or offers could be provided that had much higher returns than standard mass market approaches ever could.

This personalisation means that everyone's interaction with supermarket loyalty schemes is personalised to their behaviour, their purchasing choices. And we see that this level of personalisation has become the norm for many businesses.

Service Businesses get Personalised

The old way of doing business, where you have one way of doing something for everyone, has just about disappeared. Just think about all the things we personalise now from paper to online statements, what emails we do and don't want to receive, the ring tones we customise for family and friends, the regular orders from online shops that remember what you like, and so it goes on. We are so used to this now, the enormity of it might not be so apparent. As customers, we are empowered as never before in how we want to interact, how we want to buy. We can reward organisations we like and share information and opinions about those we don't with millions of other people like us.

Personalised Giving has Barely Reached Companies Yet

So we are empowered in all these ways but most companies still restrict giving to their favoured causes and do not allow customers and staff to support the causes of their choice. This is the old way of doing things and will naturally follow the trends I've just outlined. This is changing and I'm delighted to be part of that change as it will make a positive difference to businesses.

There are some examples worth mentioning though. Waitrose has done an amazing job in their green chip community programme. "Each month every Waitrose branch donates £1,000 (£500 in convenience shops) between three local good causes that you choose. At the checkout, you'll receive a token. Just place it in a box of the good cause you'd most like to support. The more tokens a cause gets, the bigger the donation they receive."

I really like the fact that that Waitrose has encouraged inclusivity and local organisations to be involved in this great scheme. However, it still limits choice and I look forward to seeing how it evolves over time to increase customer empowerment and personalised choice, which can only be better for Waitrose, their customers and the community in the long run.

Personal Empowerment Affects Giving in General Too

Most Giving is Currently Reactive

When we see the statistics about how much a population has given to good causes in a particular year, it always makes me cringe a bit to be honest. Most giving is in response to an 'ask' and often these 'asks' just play on guilt or fear in some way. In a commercial business, you get a response to a marketing campaign for example, so do many charities and there's little difference.

Therefore, most giving is in response to a direct request. This could be via a television advert, sponsorship, fundraising event, or it could be someone with a collecting tin. These requests raise hundreds of millions a year in the UK and those charities and schools that do this rely on this form of fundraising but it reminds me of the early days of the internet. The donors are like the early consumers of information. They are evolving to make informed choices and become more proactive in their choices of who to give to.

The choice of which cause to support is almost always taken out of our hands in these cases. Someone else has already chosen where they want your money to go. It gives an advantage to those who have the resources to get in front of you vs. those who don't. If I gave you some money right now and asked you to give it away, what cause would you choose?

Proactive Giving is on the Rise

There are a growing number of ways in which those who want to give can make informed choices about where to make an impact. I know that I have used an online system to use peer-to-peer lending to help fund development projects in developing countries. Peer-to-peer enables lots of individuals like you and me to lend small amounts to lots of other people. It's another 'many-to-many' system. No longer am I just waiting for the next organisation to ask me to give to them, I can go out and proactively choose to make that difference where I want to. As you might expect, I use TheGivingMachine to support East Herts YMCA as well as our children's school.

The internet has become a place where we can research and find out about so many great organisations and projects that we can support. This will be the big trend because people will just expect that and will want the same level of empowerment and personalisation in their giving behaviour as it evolves to be the norm in other areas of their lives.

In our home, my wife and I have encouraged our children to do the same. They are given pocket money and 10% of this is used as 'giving' money. They choose where this 'giving' money goes. We encouraged them to take their time and think about it and so James (aged eight) sponsors a tiger and Alexandra (aged twelve) sponsors a rescue dog called Rocky. It was great to see how empowered they felt to make the difference they wanted to make. I know of quite a few parents who are doing the same as well.

This is a Great Opportunity for Your Business

You can't control what people think of your organisation, its products, services or its people. However, you can influence them with what you do and how you do it. Linking these trends to the operation of your business will tap into deep and powerful forces and trends.

Many businesses will just focus on the pure commercial aspects and consider customers and staff as simply databases or resources to be segmented, sliced and diced to maximise return on investment. But those that see how the elements I have outlined come together and can be connected profitably to their organisations will have a massive advantage over those that don't.

Let's just recap these elements:

- People want to make a positive difference to their communities and beyond

- People want to choose where and how to make that difference

- People will like you and be happier if you help them do these things

Reading them, it is very, very simple but if you can engage with your customers on these points, you have a far more meaningful relationship than just a basic commercial one with limited loyalty. That's what Givenomics is all about.

The Human Desire to Belong, Contribute and Thrive

"Belong, Contribute and Thrive" Origins and Impact

East Herts YMCA

Several years ago via my work with TheGivingMachine, I met Robert Purcell, the chief executive, from East Herts YMCA (EHYMCA). Although the charity was one of many we were supporting, it was very local and so it was great to meet and get to know some of the local organisations on a personal level. Robert really impressed me with his vision and commitment to make a better world by focusing his efforts on young people in the Bishop's Stortford area.

At its core, EHYMCA provides a safe place to live for young people, many of whom have a number of issues to deal with that might be related to drugs, family relationships, crime, mental health to name but a few. As I got to know Robert, I was asked whether I'd like to become a trustee and help with their work and so after an induction period, I was approved onto the board at the charity and still serve as a trustee and Vice Chair.

The vision of the EHYMCA includes the phrase to "belong, contribute and thrive" which is part of the overall YMCA movement's vision too. They are powerful words that could apply to everyone and underpin many drivers and trends we see around us.

Consider the Opposites

I was invited to speak at the University of York and as part of that talk, I mentioned the desire for all of us to belong, contribute and thrive, and asked everyone to consider the opposites for a short while.

The opposite of belong was a state of being excluded, ostracised, unwanted, redundant.

The opposite of contribute was a state of being or feeling worthless, ignored or withdrawn.

The opposite of thrive was a state of being (or feeling) a failure or inadequate.

By looking at the opposites, the words triggered incredibly negative feelings for me and when I have known friends or family (my children for example) who are in any of these negative states, I want to help them get back into the positive state of being.

Most people would feel that way – we have in-built desires to do things that bring about a feeling of belonging, contributing and thriving. For a number of the young people that the EHYMCA serves however, their early life experiences have deeply affected their own perception of their ability to ever experience the positive aspects of these words rather than their opposites.

Belong, Contribute and Thrive Applies to us all

When I look back at my personal and business life over a number of years, I think that these words are incredibly relevant. I'd almost start backwards and look at what conditions did I need in order to feel successful or to thrive. It was always in situations or places where I could really contribute in some way and in those situations, I always belonged to something and had a strong positive feeling about that connection.

I recall moving around a great deal as a child and so I was initially an outsider in the communities we moved to. There was a strong desire to belong as quickly as possible.

This feeling is no different to starting a new company or joining a new team.

As I got more experience and took on more senior roles, I realised that enabling others who worked around me to feel that sense of belonging to a group, a team, or a company was a very powerful motivator too. Creating a climate where people felt that they were empowered to contribute and could then thrive, be and feel successful, had a massive impact on all aspects of work life from just the pleasure of being there to the actual performance results.

One of my parents' neighbours called Walter once said something to me that I have never forgotten. We were talking about how people often get to a stage in their work life where they start taking on voluntary roles in their spare time. Although he thought that this was great, his observation was that if only companies could harness the energy these people put into outside pursuits, it would make such a difference.

The people were obviously driven to contribute and thrive in a way that their companies could not support and so they needed to belong to another community to do it.

When I look around, I see:

- Millions and millions of people joining social networks because they can belong and contribute

- Day centres providing that sense of belonging to elderly people who have no other avenue

- Self help groups forming to attract those that feel

excluded to belong, contribute and thrive in their own way

And so on.

The Relevance to Companies

Given that these words can be a vision statement for everyone, the knowledge of how they can inspire and motivate the people in and around a business becomes powerful. After all, it is rare that any company has anything truly unique as a product or service that can't (or won't) be copied, replicated by someone else. Therefore, the single biggest asset is almost always the people and the way in which they work together and connect to customers, suppliers and other stakeholders.

Ensuring that an employee's ability to feel a part of something, to belong, to feel able and motivated to contribute and that their efforts are recognised, leads to feelings of success and thriving. I know that none of this is news, but by looking at it from the point of view of the individual, many will find a way to satisfy those basic needs outside the work environment anyway. However, if they have the opportunity to do so within the work environment to a greater or lesser degree, then that energy, that desire to make a difference benefits a company too.

I think that the real value comes from using a Givenomic perspective to look at relationships with customers and suppliers and other stakeholders. Seeing how simple, small changes could tap into the belong, contribute, and thrive drivers within these relationships is where the real impact of Givenomics comes in. Operating a commercial business that is successful because it engages and inspires employees, customers and other stakeholders to make a positive difference to the communities we live and work in would make everyone happy, from the finance director to employees and customers.

The Drive to Belong

Increasing Physical Isolation

I want to explore some of the more personal aspects of 'belong, contribute and thrive'. Understanding them well on a personal level can be applied to employee or customer behaviour. This leads to a better understanding of Givenomics.

The way we live today has massively changed from the way we lived in the past. As we know, it is far more common to have moved away from the communities we grew up in as children. Do you still stay in touch with or see on a regular basis people that you went to school with? Do you even know most of the neighbours around you?

It is not hard to see that if you work in a business at a business location with colleagues, that this becomes the primary community that you are part of. It will therefore be the one main community that you look for that sense of belonging to come from.

For those who work from home or are remote, lone workers, that sense of isolation is very hard to deal with. I've been in that situation myself and know what a difference being in an office with others makes.

The Rise of Alternative Places to Belong

While current trends create barriers to being able to belong on a physical level, the desire to belong drives people to find other ways to satisfy this need. Social networks have seen a massive increase in usage and are being used by so many people for so many reasons.

Just look at the growth of Facebook (below) to get an idea of how the desire to belong drives us to join in.

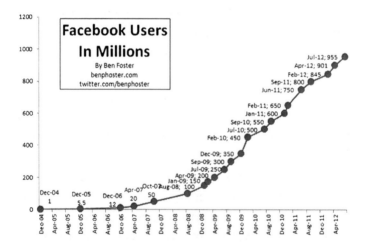

Figure 8: Facebook Growth

My father-in-law, Michael, signed up to a social network a few years ago despite being one of the last people I would ever have expected to take to the home computer revolution. He found several people that he had done national service with many years ago and not only stays in touch with them regularly but has met up with those still in the UK.

The groups within these networks and many others are flourishing as people join them to belong to groups of people with a common interest.

Community is Alive but it has Changed

For many people who are not working in offices, are retired or elderly, the massive change in their communities and indeed the world around them further increases the feeling of being physically isolated. You only have to look at local day care centres and talk to staff there to get an insight into this area.

However, the growth of, and in many cases ubiquitous access to, the internet combined with the rise in people belonging to social networks, has changed the notion of community from a purely physical one to a combination of the physical and non-physical or virtual one.

Recently, I was talking to a trustee of a local day care centre that was planning on training some of the elderly clients to use social media networks. They want to develop a buddy system to ensure that, by learning the basics, day care clients could communicate and keep an eye on each other. I look forward to seeing how that goes over the next few years. It just shows that for many, where they may feel physically isolated, internet technology combined with online communities can make a massive difference to the feeling of belonging.

It's very much the same in the workplace, where social networks are now being used inside companies, albeit with additional security and privacy to ensure internal communications and information stay private. It's the same story in that it helps create a way to belong first, which then leads on to how people can then contribute and thrive.

A Business Perspective

In addition to the example above where internal social networks for businesses are growing in popularity, how could this apply to a business in a wider sense? Since by now, you know I'm keen to consider the whole business ecosystem, I'm thinking of how it applies to customers. Customers want to belong and so it makes sense to enable those that want it to belong in some way to a community that is connected to your business.

As an example, see the image below that relates to an incredibly popular Facebook page.

Figure 9: Cadbury Creme Egg on Facebook

Clearly, all these people felt compelled to say that they wanted to be part of this grouping on a social network. How could a company create that desire to do the same? The discussion and proposition on this page is not primarily about the product – it's about the feeling, the emotion. Tapping into that is what it's all about and doing so in a way that is hard-wired to your business will make it more successful.

The Drive to Contribute

Being Needed is Part of the Story

To best understand how important this driver is, I'm going to consider a couple of examples where the opposite is the case or appears to be the case.

In the first instance, I'll use the example of someone who has been made redundant. Although I have not personally experienced this, I have supported friends through this traumatic stage in their lives. Regardless of the logic behind why the company no longer requires them, there is a deep issue that relates to being wanted. Statistics show how dangerous this feeling is if they do not secure another role quickly. Another way of saying this is that the feeling of being unwanted, unable to contribute anywhere is very damaging if it goes on too long.

I also see and hear the same story from my work with East Herts YMCA. Many of the young people have not had that feeling of being really needed or wanted within their own families, social groups and, perhaps, never or rarely in a workplace setting. For them, it might feel that their community and indeed the world in general has no place for them. It affects their perception of themselves and their approach to life.

It is a big transformation for someone who has experienced long periods of being, or feeling, unwanted to get to a position where they *do* feel wanted and able to contribute. It often involves other people and influences at the right time. It is not usually a straight path and it is common to fall back a number of times before really moving forward.

These experiences are much the same for retired people too. Unless there is a plan to belong and contribute somewhere else, all their best intentions to relax and take it easy could be overpowered by feelings of being unwanted.

It goes without saying that if the opposite is such a big issue, the human need to be wanted for their contribution is a huge, emotional driver for people. When I say people, I'm including employees, customers, suppliers and anyone else involved in a business economy.

Making a Difference is the Second Part

So you feel that you belong somewhere and your contribution is wanted. That's great. The real final piece is to feel that your contribution is making a difference. In the business context, that's all about recognition and rewards and I know many human resources people who have implemented great ways to do this.

Incidentally, I can't resist having a quick diversion here to note that in a world where we see that people want to have more emotional and personalised connections to the environment around them, the move from 'personnel' to 'human resources' is a disaster. Something relating to people, a person has now just become a resource. It sends out a terrible message of value and puts people on the same level as other resources.....[end of diversion...].

But if we widen the consideration of 'making a difference' to a much bigger picture, we see something else. The rise in the number of people volunteering in community organisations like charities and schools, the amount of donations raised during national fundraising events is staggering. People using 'bags for life', recycling, responding to disaster appeals and working on conservation projects, are all examples where people are taking actions to make a positive difference to the communities they live and work in and beyond. Much of this motivation to make a difference has been helped by a growing awareness of wider issues facing our communities, our country and the world in general. There is a growing understanding that individual actions do make a difference.

Giving Makes us Happier

I discovered a really interesting study by social psychologist Elizabeth Dunn from the University of British Columbia in Vancouver, Canada. She was looking at what kind of spending makes us happy. In an experiment she gave a certain amount of money to two groups of people. One group was given the money to spend on themselves and the other group were asked to give it away to a cause of their choice. She asked the people taking part to describe how happy they were at the beginning of the day before they were given the money and then at end of the day.

While those who received a gift of money to spend on themselves were temporarily happier than they were before, it soon wore off and they were not appreciably happier at the end of the day.

However, those who were given the same amount of money to give away to a favourite cause were appreciably happier at the end of the day. On a purely logical, economic level, this can't be right. One group is financially better off than another and yet this has not increased their happiness. The other group is not any financially better off and in fact, has to go to the bother of selecting a cause to give to yet they feel happier at the end of the day.

This result and others like it are actually hugely important when you think about it. We are conditioned to think that the acquisition of material goods and wealth leads to happiness and wellbeing, yet this is clearly not the whole picture by a long way.

The other interesting thing about this result is that we must distinguish between giving money that is yours, where you have a choice whether to give it away or not, and giving money that was given to you to give, as it were.

If you have the choice, our social conditioning means that we will have to make a judgment about whether we can afford to give or indeed should give. It might feel irresponsible to give more of your own money if you might have need of it today or tomorrow.

However, if you are enabled to give away money that would never have come to you anyway, it becomes a gift with no conflict and that's really interesting. It's interesting because that's exactly what Givenomics is all about. Not only can its benefit be measured by cashflow to community organisations as well as inbound company performance, it has the potential to increase the happiness of everyone involved.

Impact on a Company

So picture a company as a place where you enable staff and customers and possibly other stakeholders to feel a sense of belonging to something bigger than just buying your products and services. They all feel they are contributing in their own ways and that they are making a difference.

This feeling of contribution, of making a difference via a Givenomic model (ie. to the causes of their choice) has the opportunity to make stakeholders happier. This change of outlook and impact will be associated with your brand, your company and others like your company who also want to behave in this way. Just think of how empowering and motivational that is. And even better, it is totally connected to the commercial objectives of your business not just a 'bolt on' project that has a separate cost/benefit discussion.

Your customers will want to talk about your company and spread the word about what a great company it is. Price sensitivity might not be the biggest issue as it was in the past. I already know that for many shoppers, being part of something where they can buy the products they want from businesses that want to help them make a difference to their causes is more important than price alone – I can see the data every day in TheGivingMachine statistics.

Thriving as a Continual Outcome

Belonging + Contributing = Thriving

Thriving is just the positive outcome of knowing that your contribution is valued and you feel successful. It is of course an ongoing emotion and so it is never a particular place, rather a feeling of being. It therefore benefits from constant and regular triggers to engender that feeling in people.

That's why the short status messages that TheGivingMachine sends out with every donation generated are so important. It really does not matter whether a donation is for a few pennies or many pounds, it's the fact that someone bothered to make a difference. The confirmation that it has been noted and appreciated conveys the feeling of success back to the originator.

Again, I could stray into group dynamics and how regular confirmation of contribution and validation to people in a company setting or a community setting is important but there are many books and articles that cover these. I'm really sticking to how it works in a Givenomic model. With the technology platforms and the social networks available, the ability to support the communication of success, of making a difference at a basic level, has never been easier.

An Example: Inside a Company

Around 1998, I was two years into building a start-up called NorthPoint Communications. As a founder, I was really concerned with how the rapid rise of employees was affecting the overall culture. In particular, our effectiveness as a group of people working together was sliding. I was Vice President – Engineering, and while it might seem strange that this was one of my main concerns, most of my previous experience had been as a team leader leveraging team members who weren't directly reporting to me. I had to develop and use whatever personal skills I could to enable others to want to make my project a success, even though their own line managers may not have shared my goals or priorities.

It was an incredibly useful experience, although I can't say that I always appreciated it as such at the time. In order to help build a bigger sense of belonging and sense of contribution, my team and I decided to buy $5 coffee vouchers and at every team meeting, one of the agenda items was to nominate someone in another group to be awarded this as a thank you for excellent work.

Looking back on it now I can see why it worked really well on a number of levels. The recipient was always delighted to receive recognition for their contribution. It wasn't of large monetary value, but just making the effort had a huge, positive impact.

There was never a problem in someone volunteering to be the team representative to visit the person and hand it over on our behalf. The team members really enjoyed this task.

In our team meeting, having an agenda item every week that had a thank you element to it changed the flavour and feeling of the meeting at that point. Like all team meetings, there were issues and frustrations to deal with, but ending on an external focus of thanks had a huge, positive difference to the sense of belonging and contribution we felt towards each other.

Little did I really think about it at the time but it was a small example of applying Givenomics at a team level and, for $5 a week, it achieved a great deal in so many ways. I was fortunate to have a great team of people to work with who were not only excellent at their jobs but totally understood and supported these kinds of activities that had such an impact well beyond our own team.

An Example: it Works with Customers too

I've covered the way Givenomics works via TheGivingMachine previously, but I wanted to be quite specific here in terms of how the continual feeling of 'thriving' can be supported in this model. By confirming and thanking customers for making a difference when they transact with your company, you are reinforcing that behaviour, helping them to feel successful in their goal of making a difference and as the previous study shows, potentially helping customers to feel happier.

This can be extended to supporters who have already registered their intent to support particular causes but who have not generated any recent donations. They can be included in the thank you communications when payments are made to causes because they actually already stated an intent to support that cause.

The great thing about this approach is that you can help engender a feeling of success, of thriving, with a much larger audience in an inclusive way that reinforces the behaviour of those that are active and invites those that have been inactive to get more involved or to remember to use this method to support their causes when they are able to.

Givenomics connects to customer motivation to make a difference when they purchase and, being able to feel successful in that ongoing personal mission, is a key part of how Givenomics works best.

Givenomics for Customers

Customers are People Too

The word 'customers' is just segment of the people who have bought from you and it is easy to look at any group and see the statistics: their average spend, their average transaction frequency and so on. But customers are individuals too and Givenomics enables a personal preference to get involved in the transaction chain, much like any other preferences enabled via transaction sites today.

What Cause Would You Support?

Most people are quite clear about what cause they support and why. I know in my family, a combination of leukaemia, Alzheimer's and cancer research are popular as the issues they are tackling have, and still do, affect us. Talking to friends and neighbours, similar stories come forth about premature birth-related charities, children's hospital charities, hospices, as well as many others.

In building TheGivingMachine, we have seen a great wave of people supporting schools –mostly primary schools, as there are so many more compared with secondary and other teaching establishments. It can be argued that there is a vested interest in supporting your own child's school, but it is great to see the passion and energy with which a few people use to make such a difference within a community for their children and the children of so many other families too.

The really important thing is the diversity of causes that any group of people would choose to support if they could freely support any cause of their choice. That freedom to choose is at the heart of Givenomics and why it is so powerful a mechanism to go right down to the individual. That inclusivity is, after all, similar to what the founders of the internet wanted to foster in the first place.

Giving for Free Becomes a Gift

When you can give something for free such as using your time or behaviour to generate a donation for a cause, it becomes a gift and not a transaction. There was no choice about keeping the money for yourself; it was a purely altruistic gift.

This changes the whole psychology around the donation event. For me the word 'donation' has a transactional feel to it, probably because almost all donations are financial transactions and have the same mechanics as buying something. In a Givenomic model, giving is a by-product of doing something that you already do. Being acknowledged for it is more akin to holding the door open for someone and receiving thanks for it. You didn't have to do it and the world would not have stopped if you didn't, but it is somehow a better place because you did.

Givenomics Affects the Buying Decision

There are a number of factors that will affect why individuals will choose to buy a product or service from one company vs. another. Price will usually be a main factor – especially nowadays with so many ways to compare prices online, via a mobile etc. The introduction of a Givenomic model introduces another factor into the mix.

For some, the fact that they can give for free with the transaction will just be a 'nice to have'. However, from the experiences I've seen with TheGivingMachine, there are also some for whom the free giving aspect is one of the most important factors and clearly affects their buying decision. For these people, price sensitivity has been reduced because their primary influencer in where to buy from has been the Givenomics factor.

Behaviour Change vs. Financial Outcome

Are Small Amounts Worth It?

Some of the donations generated via TheGivingMachine are very small – in the order of a penny or so. The interesting thing is that sometimes there might be a few days delay in showing these donations on TheGivingMachine reports. In some cases, givers will call in or email queries relating to where those donations are and whether there are any problems with donation tracking.

The fact that someone is bothering to make that difference and then check up shows that this means a great deal to them and that they really care about converting their behaviour into another donation. That's why the real measure of success is as much the number of donations generated as it is the measure of individual choices that people made to make a difference. Some of those differences have an outcome of lots of money and some have an outcome of not so much, but they all represent a proactive choice to make a difference.

Celebrate the Behaviour

The great thing about the giving events that Givenomics encompasses is that they are ideal to share via social media. As I discussed in the previous section, it is the behaviour that is important and so I would concentrate on the event and who the giver supports more than I would on the financial outcome.

In this way, that information becomes far more inclusive and not merely an indication of wealth or the amount spent; it is a declaration, a celebration of someone making a difference and by sharing it, there is the opportunity to inspire others to take up the same behaviour to make an even bigger collective difference.

New Giving Norms

Most giving is via direct donation of one sort or another and while it is very effective, it has a major drawback in that at some point the amount people can give will be 'maxed out'. In many articles I've seen on changing giving behaviour, there are so many new ways to give but most are finding new ways to get people to part with *their* money.

The Givenomic model is one where the money comes from the commercial companies who have adopted this way of doing business and make giving a by-product of just doing what they do. It enables every customer to become a giver. By making a default cause and saying to customers that there will be a default giving event supporting this cause or, if they wish to make the choice, it can go elsewhere, a purchaser becomes a giver no matter what.

The opportunity to enable one person to generate multiple giving events on a daily basis really does create new giving norms and has a significant effect on how commercial businesses, causes, staff and people collaborate to make this happen.

Rewarding Giving Behaviour

The Scenario

So let's assume that your company has adopted a Givenomic model. It sells widgets and for every widget your customers buy, you are giving away a small percentage to good causes. As a default option, you would give that away to a favoured charity perhaps of the company. Your company, however, enables customers to choose the causes of their choice should they wish to do so.

To keep it simple, let's say that your widgets cost £20 and you are giving away 2% as part of this plan. Each widget sale generates £0.40 as a donation. It would be great if this were higher but I'm using a realistic potential value and one that is well under the average I've seen in my work on TheGivingMachine.

Thank You

Once a sale has been made, there is naturally a confirmation sent to the customer from the retailer. Now that the purchaser is also a giver, the company can thank them for giving and confirm which cause the retailer is giving to on the customer's behalf. This is a good opportunity not just for purchase confirmation but also to be more engaging and personalised.

This simple communication confirms that the customer has made a difference and reminds them of that action and that buying from a particular company caused it to happen. It's also a great time to ask customers if they would spread the word and help give away even more.

By tying a company's success to benefitting customers' causes, there is an aligned reason to generate more business.

Thank You from the Causes

Ideally, causes themselves should periodically thank the givers who have actively changed their shopping behaviour to support their cause. This is often based around donation payments but it would not have to be. Our experience to date is that despite being asked to, many charities and schools do not take the time to say thank you. The ones that do are typically the more successful ones.

TheGivingMachine has reports that show each cause where its donations have come from and some of these are public reports and so that information can be shared via social media. Company communications people can easily be on the lookout for these opportunities to share the good news.

In addition, there should be a public page that automatically reports what a company's Givenomic statistics are. That would show how many purchases (and therefore donations) had been made, how much had been raised, which causes had benefited and by how much in terms of donation numbers and, perhaps, value. This is all great information to share with a wider audience.

An example from East Herts YMCA's page on TheGivingMachine is given below.

Figure 10: East Herts YMCA on TheGivingMachine

Spreading the Word

I've already described several pages and communications that would be relevant and mention your company in a Givenomic model. All these are newsworthy and easily enhanced to enable you to share them with your entire audience of customers and staff. Each purchasing event becomes a giving event and is therefore much more likely to be shared and re-shared by your audience.

Buying a widget is not necessarily great news. Buying a widget and generating a free donation for Cancer

Research UK, Mandeville Primary School, or East Herts YMCA is far more personal and relevant and unique enough to celebrate. More importantly, it connects your company and its products in a constant stream of events.

Measuring Impact

One of the many great attributes of Givenomics is that it is measurable since the giving element is directly connected to purchasing events in this example. The social media sharing and connectivity back to your website, for example, is all easily tracked and measured. There are numerous packages and mechanisms to track origination of referring websites or emails.

The resultant public relations benefits are a little harder to quantify as return on investment. There will always be some element of PR aspect to consider and I know that previously I've measured PR impact as column inches written about a company, topic or product in the wider media in previous roles. Ultimately, it is sales that companies need to drive, and that's what the bottom line measures.

From a customer perspective, they can measure their impact too and that is easily quantified with the same kind of metrics – number of donations generated and the resulting amount of donation value generated.

I'm an average online consumer and I give an additional £200 or more a year using this model. This can be verified, measured, tracked and reported. My chosen causes can contact me about how that money makes a difference to the communities and/or causes they serve.

Implementing Givenomics for a Business

I've touched on some of the benefits to a business (possibly your business) across the previous chapters, but I wanted to pull all the information together into one place to enable a business owner or leader to get a full picture of how it connects and works.

TheGivingMachine has given me most of the core experience over the last few years to draw upon and so I'll use examples and numbers based on practice. I'll cover the following areas:

- The scenario
- Brand differentiation
- Ongoing costs
- Marketing opportunities
- Corporate giving
- Business to business opportunities

In general, I have focused on a business to consumer model because that is where my work with TheGivingMachine has provided the most experience to draw upon, but there are also ways to leverage Givenomics into a business-to-business model too.

The Scenario

Setting the Commission

I'm going to share with you the set up scenario of how we built TheGivingMachine. This will give you an idea of what I would suggest you do if you need or want to do this on your own for your business.

Firstly, you would set a percentage shared per transaction. Some of the retailers TheGivingMachine works with have different percentages depending on what type of goods they sell. This relates to the differing margins that are made on goods, so if you have a system that can do that too, that would be great.

The gross commission marked for this scheme could range from 1% to 5%, for example, depending on product line profit margins.

In TheGivingMachine model, 25% of this gross commission is retained to cover the costs of tracking and distributing the monies raised for customer chosen causes as well as to maintain the website and provide all the reports. The remaining 75% is converted into the donation and these net donation values are the ones displayed on the website.

Setting a Default Giving Option

Some customers won't want to bother making a choice about where to give. They may not have the time or the inclination to choose at that time. Setting a default cause option is a great way to enable every purchase to be a giving event.

Online Customer Preferences

Online, it is slightly easier to implement Givenomics with a default cause to give to. If a customer wishes to register a preference to where the donations they have generated go, then they will need to be able to select the causes they want to support. You'll need a way for them to search and choose which causes to support. In TheGivingMachine scenario, if their cause is not listed, then it can be nominated manually by the giver. In our case, it has to be a valid charity or school but you might choose a wider remit. The only thing I would be concerned with is the sheer number of other organisations that you would have to have vetted and the associated resources needed for assessment.

Finally, it is worth mentioning inclusiveness. While it may seem natural to enable a giver to support just one cause, TheGivingMachine's design enables people to support up to four in any percentage split. To be fair, very few people use all four slots available but a significant number use more than one. Just imagine parents with children in two schools or people who want to support a school and a charity for example. It would be better to enable this inclusivity from the start rather than enforce exclusivity.

Offline Customer Preferences

This would most likely have to be done via some form of loyalty card or registration scheme so that every purchase still made a donation to a default beneficiary, unless you took out a loyalty card there and then which you could activate when at home and go online to change the default cause. It would be a great way to incentivise and recruit loyalty programme customers. This is not an area we've implemented yet, but are reviewing those that provide these elements to see how it could be done in the future.

Donation Tracking

So now you have all the setup elements done, you would just need a sales transaction report, along with the allocated commission, which is uploaded into a donation tracking system to calculate and report which causes get which amounts. You can look at all the events by the customer that generated them, by the cause that is going to receive them, by event date, type etc.

Reconciliation and Payment

The reconciliation is fairly easy, at some point there will be an allocation of commissions transferred into your account for the Givenomic model and then you'll just need to allocate the right amount of funds to the right causes and pay them out.

This is where the Givenomic model really benefits from using a partner because setting up the bank payment details with the right amount of due diligence and carrying them out for hundreds of payments is quite a task and benefits from economies of scale.

TheGivingMachine recently sent out a monthly payment of about £40,000 to over 1,000 causes, for example, and this is rising.

If you restricted the number of causes one could support, then that might alleviate this problem but it would become more exclusive and, for me, that veers away from the true Givenomic model. It has to be inclusive and not exclusive.

Brand Differentiation

Brands have More Value than Products

Business leaders know that a brand is one of the most important assets you are building with a business. Of course the products and services are important too but if you interact with many customers, even that interaction is part of your brand. These attributes will outlive most specific products and services that you offer.

Consumers are becoming much more aware of issues in their communities and further afield due to the increased media attention on everything from sustainability and global warming effects to poverty and natural disasters. They are naturally becoming more and more aware of how some brands relate to these issues. Which companies are part of the problem, which are part of the solution and which are just not participating? If you are a business owner, what does your brand stand for?

Givenomics leverages customer choices about where to make a difference and links it to their buying behaviour. It supports a brand by demonstrating that it cares about what customers care about and one that is committed to making a difference. This is great brand differentiation and will constantly evolve; furthermore, you can track that evolution and make it part of your brand messaging.

Keeping it Fresh

Since the exact customer mix will vary significantly (ie. you don't have the same people buying from you constantly), buying events will generate continually changing giving events. This information can be aggregated and is ideal for sharing in a social media setting and so is reporting on where donations are going to and what types of causes are most popular at that time.

If you have a company that has outlets in different regions or you have customers who can be segmented geographically, even this can be used to build a giving map of your customers and what causes they connect to. This is great brand differentiation material that is dynamic and will stay fresh all the time with the right data systems behind it.

Engendering Brand Advocacy

By associating the giving outcome with buying from your company, you have also given your customer a great reason to become a brand advocate to their friends and family. In the model TheGivingMachine implemented, customers receive a thank you after purchases have been made that triggers them to check an updated donation report. The shop names are in this report as well as the amounts raised. It is another reinforcement message that associates a brand with supporting their causes. This then helps the customer to think much more positively about the business that they have bought from.

The Ongoing Costs are Fixed

Controlling Costs

There are two main costs to the business to run a Givenomics programme. Firstly there are the costs of the giving element (the commission/donation) and secondly, there are costs associated with the tracking and distribution of the donations generated. I wouldn't include the marketing and PR costs as these should really be part of any programme a business undertakes to engage with its audience. It is the incremental, programme-specific costs that I want to concentrate on.

As I've already covered in the earlier scenario, the giving element is fully controlled and is directly tied to the amount of product or services sold. Therefore, it should be costed into the sale price and not really be an addition. Depending on the kind of business you operate, some products and services may have higher margins than others. This therefore gives rise to a potential range of percentages or amounts given per sale.

Some of the shops on TheGivingMachine use a fixed sum giving element and some use a percentage of sale price. As long as it is a reasonable amount, it represents the philosophy of 'it's the thought that counts'. If you can afford to give away a large amount or percentage, the first thought that any savvy customer is going to have is that you are making too much margin!

The tracking and distribution element is a bit harder to quantify in terms of value but there are other organisations that could help with that aspect. Apart from approaching TheGivingMachine to do that, the Charities Aid Foundation may also be able to help with this aspect too for distributing funds to charities. There are a few commercial businesses that use similar functionality to TheGivingMachine and they may be able to help on the tracking and distribution aspect. Typically, they are not social enterprises and will have shareholders and profit motivations to satisfy too.

Either way, there are choices but building your own tracking or distribution mechanism would not necessarily be cost effective. What you really need for your PR, marketing and communications is access to the data and the ability to generate various reports from it.

Givenomics Represents Controlled Risk

There is always a setup cost with any programme but by keeping it simple to start with, the ongoing financial exposure is controlled. In the unlikely event that customers or staff do not respond well to the initial call to action, the business is not committed to massive 'prizes'. Whether it builds slowly and gains momentum or whether it goes with a bang, the risk is controlled.

I know that for many businesses the economic climate has made them risk averse. They may behave in an over-cautious manner – we all are affected by the collective mood of the communities we are part of, whether they be work or personal ones. Even though I am passionate about growing awareness of using Givenomics to benefit all stakeholders, looking at the concept from a purely financial and business perspective is important because the concept must be able to stand up to basic commercial scrutiny.

Whether your implementation is a small pilot followed by a national/international rollout or is full-on from the beginning, the costs directly relate to the success in terms of sales and I would suggest that there are not many marketing programmes that can say that.

Marketing Benefits of Givenomics

Givenomics in Marketing

There are plenty of examples of a giving element in marketing consumer goods. Everything from charity Christmas cards to specially selected packs of baked beans. There is always a story around the end of the year about the exact amount of donation money that goes to charity from greetings cards as there seems some doubt in the public's mind about that.

These all work well in their own right to a greater or lesser degree, but they are not part of a Givenomic model for me. They are exclusive to the charity partnerships chosen by the retailer or product brand. This exclusivity will work well for some charities that have a more universal appeal. It is this very exclusivity that keeps the opportunity constrained and unable to fully engage an audience.

The motivation changes from:

We want to make a difference with your help

to

We want to help *you* make a difference

Just imagine how you could market your products when you say that to prospective customers. You empower them on a very deep and personal level. Just think of the follow-up PR and advertising that could happen as part of campaigns. It is much, more powerful than having to use a dissatisfaction approach.

What if Givenomics became the primary focus of an outbound engagement programme? A programme that became part of what the company and its staff stood for? There are a number of other companies already taking the first steps towards this kind of model. The Waitrose scheme I covered earlier is a terrific example but still limits choice.

The Direct Opportunity

Givenomics gives you an ability to have a bigger call to action than just 'buy my product' should you wish to leverage that. Each business would have to think about how best to go to market with a revised approach though – is it a primary message or a secondary message, for example? The call to action is to buy a product from a specific retailer because the customer will be part of something bigger – primarily centred around that company as an enabler, a catalyst for positive change. Most importantly, this change centres on the individual and empowers them to be the most important player in this change.

This last aspect is inspiring and gives rise to many opportunities to use stories of normal, everyday people who make a difference to support so many different causes. Linking a brand with that becomes amazing, positive and sustainable, going forward. It becomes less and less about what a company has achieved. It becomes a message about what customers have achieved with the company. Instead of *me*, it becomes *us* – a much more inclusive approach.

The personalisation down to the level of the individual is an important part of this approach: everyone can see the impact as part of the bigger picture, but to be able to drill down to the individual level and to thank people for their contribution has an even greater effect. I have a great friend, Patrick, who is also a fellow trustee of East Herts YMCA. Patrick is adamant that he does not want to receive thank you messages from TheGivingMachine or charities but I know from feedback, observation and more rigorous research from others, that this is not the prevailing view. Most people want acknowledgement or, at the very least, to know that their efforts have been counted in some way.

That acknowledgement is a perfect direct communication opportunity with customers. This could be via an online acknowledgement but it can take place at the point of sale too, on a till receipt, for example.

The Indirect Opportunity

The community organisations that have benefitted, or will benefit, from a company adopting a Givenomic model can also play a part in the marketing aspects. For many companies, being involved with charitable giving elements usually represents picking a major partner. This may still be the case, but there is an opportunity to highlight and involve a few of the many thousands of smaller organisations making a difference on the ground in communities across the UK.

If I look at the work of the East Herts YMCA or Supporting Dalit Children (a small charity set up in 2008 to educate Dalit children, the 'untouchables', in Southern India), they are unlikely to ever be adopted by a large, national company as a charity of the year as they are too small and focused. However, they could easily be contenders for being featured in a montage of organisations that are directly impacting vulnerable people. These smaller, locally run organisations do not have access to the larger fundraising and awareness opportunities that bigger charities do. Givenomics gives them a chance to raise awareness for the fantastic work that they do and hopefully attract more support from others that share the same passion to make a difference in a particular way.

All of these organisations will have some form of outbound communication channels ranging from postal, email to full-on social media. If your company has now enabled them to receive additional funds, if supporters bought your products and services – that is news to be shared!

On a similar level, you will know, if you are a parent, that there are never enough funds in schools to do everything that you want to do, or to have access to all the play equipment or sports equipment that would enhance your child's education. Schools are always incredibly supportive of programmes that are simple to communicate and support and so they also would want to share news with parents about how their purchasing choices can have a positive impact on the school.

You can see that it would not be hard to be able to get support from many thousands of charities and schools across the UK to raise awareness of a new Givenomic model. It might start in a region and spread but either way, there is a great opportunity for indirect support of a Givenomic programme.

Marketing to Connect Emotionally and Celebrate Impact

Consider the marketing models that could help bring about more business success by using a Givenomic approach. Initially, it would be all about joining in to make a difference in ways chosen by staff and customers. Tap into the emotional desire to make a difference along with the personalised choice of that impact. There can be no hidden agendas with this, no cynicism from staff or customers about company motives. By linking your business motivation to be successful to staff and customer motivations to make a difference, the combined marketing and social benefit activity can be very open, measurable and transparently communicated.

Once the Givenomic performance metrics start rolling and you have measurements, then the marketing strategy can change to become about the stories of staff, of customers and the causes they have chosen and why. Human stories are so much more powerful to us than any corporate message. By linking your company to these messages and celebrations, staff and customers will like your company even more. They will recommend it to others and other companies will want to emulate what you have achieved and will continue to achieve.

Coming back full circle, you will be able to celebrate your business success as a collective win and not just a win for you and your shareholders. So often, it seems that businesses and business leaders need to be coy about success. Givenomics gives companies and business leaders a cause to celebrate and communicate how successful they have been and how that directly translates into having a social impact on staff, customers, communities and potentially at a global level.

Givenomics Marketing and PR Opportunities

So you've got your Givenomic model working now. In addition to your usual marketing channels, you could also leverage the third sector media as buying your products and services will directly and positively impact all the charities that have supporters who could be your customers.

The school media marketplace is now available to you, as you may also be appealing to prospects that have connections to schools such as parents and grandparents.

There are also many local community media outlets that could promote your products and services, since you would directly support the local organisations chosen by customers who are part of that community.

For example, let's say you have 10,000 transactions, each giving £1 away, and this is able to touch 3,000 different charities and schools. Just think of all the different ways that could be reported and think of the positive impact your business will have had and how customers, schools, charities and the public in general will feel about that.

Corporate Giving/Social Responsibility Sorted

Connecting to Your Business Model

So far, I have mostly focused discussion of Givenomics on the commercial aspects because I firmly believe that any strategic programme should be firmly and directly connected to commercial success criteria. The corporate social responsibility (CSR) concerns of businesses are incredibly important in this aspect too, although it is often hard for businesses to combine these objectives.

For many companies the responsibility for managing CSR sits within a HR function. In a number of sample programmes I have seen, the CSR activities will support selected charities of the year and also have external activities that support staff development, whether it is in terms of teamwork or personal development. There are few companies able to point to CSR programmes that directly connect to commercial success criteria and which involve customers as well as staff.

There is a growing sentiment among business owners that they want to connect their businesses more deeply to the communities around them. There is also the growing desire of customers to play some part in dealing with the issues that face them, their communities and the wider world too. That desire, as we have already discussed, translates into an expectation of the companies that are successful and making profits to play their part too.

Unfortunately, most CSR programmes still feel like an additional cost burden to many business owners rather than an opportunity that will positively affect their business, their staff and customers as well as the wider world around them.

Givenomics Integrates Social Responsibility

By tying the giving element of a business directly to its commercial activity, the social responsibility as well as the corporate giving aspect can arguably be said to now be integrated into the overall strategy. It's no longer a distraction or an additional item on the management team status reports on performance. I know that I've spoken to a number of company directors and typically the agenda items for CSR or giving elements are not first items up – they tend to be later ones after the company performance information like sales and financial reports.

In this way, Givenomics takes a more holistic approach to commercial success and engagement. As a result, CSR and its performance would command a high placement on management and board agendas. For those looking to find a way to achieve CSR goals linked with commercial success, they will be happy. For those that have resisted CSR activities as a distraction, they will see it as a sales and marketing strategy that has a significant upside in providing a CSR benefit as a direct consequence.

Is Charity of the Year still Relevant?

For many companies, there is a yearly activity to choose a charity of the year. For the 'winning' charity it promises some great opportunities for the year ahead. For the losing charity or charities, they will have had to spend quite a bit of time and money to put a bid together and losing represents a cost for the charity to bear. To play this game, they have to behave more and more like businesses to win business and take risks to secure income instead of concentrating on their primary objective.

By empowering customers and employees to choose the causes supported, there is less of a need for this kind of activity and perhaps, the various charities could spend their valuable resources on awareness activities instead of on bid management. Givenomics is inclusive and not exclusive.

There is still a fit for a charity of the year type scheme though, as it could be the default giving option for those that do not want to make the effort to choose something different. This would still be a great opportunity for a business and a charity to team up in some way while still empowering personal choice if and where people want to use it.

What about Business to Business?

Revising the Givenomics Model

So far, I've mostly spoken about Givenomics in a business to consumer (B2C) model. This is because I have several years' experience in building and running that model via TheGivingMachine. However, I can also see a tremendous opportunity in the business to business (B2B) model too.

There are several key differences in how that can be achieved and how it connects to commercial success but the principle is the same. I'm going to provide an overview here for consideration and I am sure there will be some great feedback and thoughts from others too.

B2B Givenomics

The overall principle is to link the behaviour that leads to commercial success with a giving outcome for the key stakeholders in that process. For a B2B business, one of the key criteria will be having effective relationships with the other businesses that are customers.

However, there are some important aspects to consider. For Givenomics to have a mass appeal and impact, it needs to have a large network value. In a B2B business, which only has a few customers, it may be difficult to maximise the network value without a change in approach.

The same principles can still apply in that a percentage of the profits can be given away to causes chosen by key stakeholders. This could be based on a per transaction basis or it could be based on a monthly or quarterly basis connected to financial reports that detail commercial performance.

It is important, though, that the giving element is seen as something that the originator is doing anyway, and that the stakeholder is helping to divert rather than as an optional part of a transaction. In this way, the giving aspect is hard wired into the commercial business and not just an optional bolt on.

B2B vs B2C Stakeholders

In the B2C model I've mainly focused on, I've outlined how consumer customers are the key stakeholder to focus on. However, in a B2B business model, it would be relatively easy to include the customer representatives who place business and your own staff.

Let's assume that we have a B2B company and it assigns a percentage of profits or revenue into a 'giving pot'. This could be done on a monthly or quarterly basis based on performance. For this to be effective, it would be best to not go any longer than this (eg. annually) as the benefit of regularly communicating with the network of stakeholders would be diminished.

The company then defines who will decide where that 'giving pot' goes to by identifying those who will get to choose. This could be a combination of staff and buyers, for example.

Just think how great the communication would be to a buyer asking them to confirm who their company would like to nominate to receive a contribution on their combined behalf? If your buyer as an individual is not very senior in their organisation, it is a great opportunity for them to get senior visibility. By contributing to their cause, it connects you to their company more effectively.

Staff members could be invited into this group too, since their contribution to the success of any company is vital and enabling them to make a difference to their chosen causes would be a great motivational and reward mechanism.

B2B Givenomic Opportunities

Compared to the B2C environment previously covered, the principles are essentially the same. By implementing a Givenomic model and including key stakeholders in its implementation, a network of connected people and organisations is built up that together celebrates commercial success with a social benefit that can work just as well in a B2B context as it does in a B2C one.

That network of people should be one that can positively influence the commercial success of a business and, in that way, Givenomics has the best chance of achieving great things. As I write this book, I'm talking to a number of organisations who are interested in this model and I look forward to sharing that information as part of my follow-up.

The other great opportunity to mention here is the multitude of business groups and organisations that would be delighted to hear from any company that has connected their business model directly to supporting its community. Most of the networks I have been invited to, or joined, have significantly more B2B businesses than B2C ones and so this avenue becomes a great avenue for promotion, sales and more impact.

Givenomics for Charities and Schools

A New Source of Sustainable Funds

Fundraising: Taking or Giving?

I'll have to come clean here on how I feel about the business of fundraising and how it relates to giving. When I first started TheGivingMachine, I went out to meet some of the bigger fundraisers to get their feedback. I approached a well-known children's charity with the concept – one that I had raised money for personally in the past. It was surprising that the feedback I received was not that positive, as their approach was all based on return on investment and how they found it more effective to ask supporters for an extra £10 a year, knowing that some would be annoyed with the request but feeling it was worth it for the end result.

I'm very comfortable with business approaches but the 'charity supporter business' could be different. I wrote a blog on this topic some time ago that asked the question whether fundraising was about giving or taking. It was clear from the many conversations that I have had that fundraising for many fundraisers is really about the efficiency of taking.

The business I wanted to build was always more about the giving side of the equation rather than the taking side. It was this experience with large fundraisers that really helped us understand that we should focus on being 'giver-centric' with TheGivingMachine above all else.

The People Connection

If you go to any business networking function and the topic of conversation turns to what people do outside of their usual day-to day-business, it may come as no surprise that many are already heavily involved in local and sometimes national causes of one kind or another. This can range from being a parent helping out at their child's school to being a trustee. You already know that I am a trustee of East Herts YMCA from earlier chapters, for example.

It's no surprise therefore that for many, seeing a way to connect these roles that has benefits for all makes sense. Although businesses, schools and charities are incredibly different in their purpose, there is an inevitable crossover of the same people involved in at least two out of the three types of organisations.

Developing an Additional Funding Stream

There are two main reasons that Givenomics can be a great source of funds from a school or charity point of view. Firstly, it provides a recurring revenue stream. Admittedly, it will vary by the time of year because spending patterns may mirror seasonality and so will the resulting donation payments.

However, most school and charity fundraising is event driven. There is a big build up to an event, a celebration of what it has achieved, a quiet time and then on to the next event. There are few mechanisms other than a straight direct debit from a supporter's bank account that enable recurring funds to be generated. These recurring payments via a Givenomic approach continue as long as supporters have joined a scheme and are using it. For example that could apply to joining and using TheGivingMachine for all online purchases (office supplies, gifts, insurance, holidays etc).

From a fundraiser's perspective, this is an easy and very welcome proposition.

The Funds are Unrestricted

Many charities and schools who raise funds from specific sources like grants or contracts, have very specific uses tied to those funds. This is to ensure that the money is used to achieve goals specified by the funder. However, funds generated by Givenomics wouldn't be restricted in this way and that would enable the various causes to use these funds in other, perhaps more creative ways.

I know for example that the East Herts YMCA has used funds generated via TheGivingMachine to fund day trips for some of the residents to have some time out, build friendships and support their personal journeys towards belonging, contributing and thriving. These activities may not qualify for external funding but can still play an important role in the development of East Herts YMCA's clients. The story will be the same for many causes – where they have some flexibility to try other projects big and small that support their core purpose.

Givenomics Makes Supporter Engagement Easier

The Usual 'Ask' is Giving Your Money

Talking to fundraisers, the term they use for the call to action is usually referred to as 'the ask'. That might be to donate £5, sponsor someone or to sign up for recurring support. As I am sure you have experienced yourself, there are many different ways and locations for this to happen. It could be in the street as you are shopping either by collecting tins or by a representative asking you to sign up to a regular commitment.

Like many others, I receive quite a few requests in the post too. Once you have supported one cause, you can then find yourself contacted by many others too. All of these requests or 'asks' are for money in a one-off payment or as ongoing support and they have worked effectively and in the same basic way since charitable giving started.

While the typical forms of fundraising do work well, most rely on using guilt as a motivator to spur people into action. The prospective supporter feels guilty and that they should do something to make a difference as they really can spare some money. One of the problems with this type of support is that it is very reactive and, while it does help causes reach fundraising goals, it does not leave much of an opportunity to have a positive impact on the giver and spur them to want to do more. In fact, the direct approach often forces people to behave in an unnaturally rude way to people who ask for donations.

My wife and I have our charitable giving set up for a number of causes. Periodically, we get phone calls from these organisations thanking us but with a real agenda to increase the amounts. If we are unable to, I interrupt the caller's script to let them know that I appreciate their call but I need to let them know that we can't increase the amount this time. In the many, many phone calls taken, all but one have said thank you and terminated the call quickly to get on to the next prospect. The clear message is that although I'm thanking you – you are not important to us unless you can increase your donation.

I was pleasantly surprised when one caller from Cancer Research UK said to me that not increasing the amount was no problem but they would still like to take a couple of minutes to let me know how and where donations like ours made a difference. I was really impressed and felt that this campaign had the giver in mind, compared to the many others that considered the taking aspect only.

Changing the 'Ask' to be About Giving for Free

The 'ask' in a Givenomic model is very different and far more positive. In Givenomics, the request is for people to make a relatively small behaviour choice, a choice to do something slightly differently to generate a positive outcome for the cause.

Typically, I always recommend that the charities and schools that have joined TheGivingMachine ask people to start giving for free and consider supporting their particular cause as one of their chosen beneficiaries. This form of 'ask' is far more positive and does not rely on guilt.

This form of request is also much more inclusive as just about everyone could join in since there is no financial cost. From a fundraiser's perspective, it becomes a much easier and less confrontational way of asking for support – especially in financially trying times where every penny counts for many people. The idea that they can carry on doing what they normally do with a slight behaviour change to benefit a cause is incredibly compelling.

Attracting New Charity Supporters

Givenomics is a great way to attract new supporters since there is a much lower barrier to overcome in order to become a supporter – just a behavioural change. A relationship can be developed with these supporters with some of them engaging more deeply, depending on their preferences and wishes.

For existing supporters, it is a great way to ask them to help a bit more without asking them for more money. Going back to the outbound phone conversations I mentioned earlier, the outcome could be very different for many charities that undertake outbound calling if the call to action was a Givenomic-based one. It would leave a much more positive feeling for all concerned and still have the potential to achieve financial goals.

The harder, direct request for more money becomes softened. I hear the same feedback from parents as well as charity supporters that repeated requests for more money can leave many feeling guilty. They feel they can't give more support or, indeed, become angry that they are being asked to do so when their financial situation or uncertainty over the future means that they can't increase their contributions.

Therefore, Givenomics provides causes with a way of asking for support or additional support that does not have the potential to impact negatively on their cause. It's a win-win.

Continuous Supporter Engagement

Typical fundraising mechanisms focus on events or signing up to recurring amounts. Either way, the supporter or donor makes a commitment at one point in time. It is then up to the cause to keep the relationship going with various communications, which should include details of the impact that supporters have made to that cause.

In a Givenomic model, the support is ongoing and hopefully continuous. In TheGivingMachine model, every online purchase generates a donation and so there is an opportunity to have a touch point on a regular basis. When payments come through (which for the active causes is monthly), there is an opportunity to thank all supporters for helping to make a difference. This regular touch point is a great way for causes to maintain a relationship based on positive news and invite additional support without using guilt as a motivator.

Fit with Existing Fundraising activities

Events

Most causes, be they charities or schools, centre fundraising efforts around events of some kind. For schools that might include fun days, Christmas shopping evenings, May Fayres or summer barbeques. Charities have their own range of events that will obviously differ depending on the charities themselves.

These events are a great time to introduce an audience already predisposed to supporting a cause to a Givenomic way of helping more. The call to action, to get involved, is much more effective in these situations. There is an opportunity to highlight those commercial companies that are participating in schemes using Givenomic approaches too.

Without labouring the point, it is much easier for the organisation hosting the event to highlight a Givenomic scheme along with the other ways to support it directly as it is inclusive and not based on how much more you are willing to donate there and then.

Post Event Follow Up

As part of a fundraising event, there will usually have been information collected on the participants – maybe just to be clear on numbers. Where names and email addresses are available, simple follow-up emails to thank people for their support will be sent out. These are also great opportunities to highlight the additional support that can be given for free via a Givenomic scheme, as well as promoting selected companies that are participating.

It may not be appropriate to ask for more financial support if people have recently paid to be at an event. However, asking attendees to give a bit more for free does not have the same issues and is likely to be received far more favourably.

New Supporters

When new supporters sign up to support a cause via donation, this can also be a great time to mention Givenomic schemes, along with associated companies, in order to increase the contribution that supporters can make on an ongoing basis. Invite these new supporters to make a small change in behaviour to generate long term impact.

Within a specific charity or school, there will be many other opportunities where new and existing supporters can be approached to let them know about a Givenomic scheme like TheGivingMachine and encourage more people to join in. The purpose of the sections above was just to give a flavour of the possibilities and how it can still relate to participating businesses.

The Power of Data

Privacy vs. Public Reporting

By enabling each purchase to become a giving activity, there is an opportunity to share it either publicly or with key stakeholders. In TheGivingMachine, we probably erred on the side of being too cautious to begin with. Everything was kept private except for the donation amounts and the particular shops involved.

It would have been possible to pass on details of supporters to the causes they support – and in some cases that information can be sold and there are many companies that do that. I think that is one of the benefits of being a social enterprise – we can be guided by what is the right thing to do, as well as by financial performance, and so we elected to make sure that contact details stay private.

However, there is an increasing desire to share personal information that pertains to your community, your friends, colleagues etc., often via social networks. Therefore, TheGivingMachine is enabling various privacy options to share as much or as little of the actual giving activities and supporter names as people want to share.

Contact is enabled from the causes to their supporters on the scheme and, in that way, supporters can be invited into other forums of direct communication on their terms. This is consistent with a 'giver-centric' approach to empower people to support who they want and in whatever way they want.

Tracking Reports

Due to the vast amount of data that is produced every month, there are some great reports available to causes that benefit from a Givenomic scheme. These reports can easily identify which commercial companies are the source of the additional funds coming in. It provides an opportunity to connect the cause to those companies or to talk about them in various supporter updates.

One example would be the contribution that office supply companies make to various causes on TheGivingMachine. There are several such companies like Viking Direct or Staples and by asking their own staff, charities, schools and other local business owners to place orders using a Givenomic scheme, these office supply companies become great sources of donations for schools and charities. This is exactly the experience I have seen around Bishop's Stortford and you can see an example below.

Figure 11: East Herts YMCA Donations

PR Opportunities for Causes

There are two main areas of PR opportunities that are enabled with this level of tracking. Firstly, high-performing supporters can be identified and personal stories of why they support a particular cause can be shared. It is always the more personal stories that can have the biggest impact on other supporters and potential supporters. I know from my own experience, there is a history of Alzheimer's disease and cancer in our family – dreadful and debilitating conditions. In addition to supporting our children's school, these are causes close to us, but talking to friends and neighbours, I have heard many, many other stories that people would share if it helped the cause in some way.

I've also talked about the link with the commercial companies supporting a Givenomic scheme. As TheGivingMachine has grown, I've seen more and more brands engaging in activities that can be linked to PR with supporters of causes and vice versa. These activities do not have to be high cost, but build brand advocacy. This also reinforces the behaviour of supporters, which in turn generates more income for the causes they support.

What If ?

Vision of a Givenomic Future

Establishing Givenomics as a Recognised Concept

A number of years ago I wrote my own personal mission statement. I had read a great book called *First Things First* by Stephen Covey (who sadly passed away while I was writing this book). One of the elements it suggests is that each of us should undertake to develop a personal mission statement. From my own experience, it's something you uncover rather than something you define – if that makes sense.

Among other things, I knew that I wanted my time on this planet to amount to a net benefit to others in some way. I have been incredibly fortunate in my life so far and that means I have a fair way to go to reach that goal. For me, one way to move the balance in the right direction is to share the concept of Givenomics. It enables businesses to be a major part of the solution. To me, it just makes sense and I hope that you find that too. I'm sharing it now as the concept is still young and can benefit from the help and contribution of people like you to become so much more and have an even greater positive impact.

In this chapter, I want to explore the 'what if' scenario of major adoption and consider what a difference that could make to us all.

The Contribution of Others

The Givenomic concept, while proven in reasonable numbers, is not yet rolled out on a massive scale. One of my intentions in writing this book is to enable people like you to add to the debate, to the opportunity to evolve the concept into the incredible force for good that it can be. I like to think of it as an open model that benefits from the contribution of others; hence why TheGivingMachine was founded as a not-for-profit social enterprise.

This contribution will help ensure that some of the key enablers are available and fit for purpose as Givenomics becomes more popular and is much more widely utilised. The platforms required to track and report data on this scale will need to be in place. This in itself is not necessarily a technical issue but is a commercial one. This concept needs a cost-effective infrastructure so that the cost to deliver does not detract from the benefit provided by giving away as much as possible.

With large-scale adoption, further economies of scale can come into play and in the case of TheGivingMachine, there will be the opportunity to retain less of the gross commission to cover costs. All of this growth can only come about with the help of others to make it happen and I can already see the pieces lining up for that future.

Unleashing the Potential

We know that giving in general is a good thing to do and makes you feel good. I know that is a rather mushy thing to say in a book that is focused on a business audience but it is true and backed up by empirical evidence from behavioural psychologists, so it's OK to feel that way!

Givenomics as a concept leverages these aspects of human psychology in a way that can be measured, tracked and reported on and, from the data I've shared, it works on a measurement and business economic level too.

This creates a huge opportunity for those combinations of commercial organisations, customers and causes that 'get it' to unleash the potential of everyone working together with a combination of individual goals, but also a common collective goal of making a difference.

Wealth Distribution Decided by the Many

I thought about that title for a while and it could come across as being anti-commercial but let's think about it for a second. You have a company that makes profit. It makes profit because your staff work hard to provide a great service or product to customers. What if a percentage of that profit was redistributed via a Givenomic model? What if both customers and staff could decide where it went? You would still have the bulk of profits to meet all the financial and return obligations but now you empower the very people who generate that profit to help give some of it away to their favourite causes.

It gives a great reason for everyone involved to want your company to be incredibly successful. In the current model that you use for your company, why would any of your staff and customers want you to be incredibly successful?

Unless staff have some kind of share option/profit sharing scheme, they will naturally tend to be primarily interested in their own career progression, on how their job benefits them and on how best to ensure their position is secure.

Why would customers care? Chances are that they can buy the same product or similar ones elsewhere. Givenomics connects your stakeholders to your company in an economic model that distributes some of the wealth they helped generate and they will love your company for it. They key has to be that *they choose*. If your company chooses the causes, it is just another corporate PR thing that most, if not all, will see through as a project tainted with a commercial goal and not a social one that connects to them.

Prosperity Should Lead to Happiness

Givenomics uses a giving approach in a way that is more business focused and which enables the prosperity of all companies to be part of a far bigger purpose – to transform communities across the globe by empowering everyone to choose how to make that difference.

Mobilising that incredible force and emotional driver and connecting directly to businesses will enable those who are prosperous to connect more deeply to the world around them through the choices of their staff and customers. The opportunity is there to link that prosperity to an increased feeling of contribution and therefore, happiness.

It would be great to see people discussing how well a company has done and the impact that it has via its customers as a function of its success, rather than the main story being focused on executive pay, shareholder revolt or staff dissatisfaction.

Quantifying the Opportunity

What if all Online Spend Used Givenomics?

To quantify a possible opportunity, I'm going to consider all online spend in the UK. According to the IMRG Capgemini e-Retail Sales Index, British online shoppers spent £68 billion in 2011, 16% more than the year before.

Since TheGivingMachine experience to date has been via an online model, this seems a sensible place to start quantifying the opportunity. If we then assume a modest 2% giving element as an average, this results in £1.36 billion a year!

If all online shopping was made via Givenomic schemes, the collective impact on community organisations would be more than £1 billion a year. Compare this to the size of some of the largest national fundraising activities like Red Nose Day 2011 for example which raised just over £100 million.

Quite apart from the much deeper connectivity between people, commercial organisations and causes, Givenomics provides a credible and sustainable scenario.

What if all Consumer Spending Used Givenomics?

While it is a growing percentage, online spending is only a part of all consumer spending. IMRG Capgemini estimate that the above online figures only represent 17% of all consumer spending. What if all spending was considered in order to scope out the opportunity? Again, looking at the UK for statistics we see the following numbers: £400 billion total spend in 2011.

Assuming a conservative average of 2% giving element, that leads to a whopping £4 billion financial impact on many thousands of causes. This impact is truly incredible and enables people, communities, commercial companies and causes to work together to make a massive difference. Even if 2% is too ambitious, halve these numbers to 1% and they are still enormous compared to the biggest fundraising events around.

What Difference Could this Actually Make?

According to an annual review of the Charity 100 Index, published in April 2012's *Charity Finance* magazine and online at Civilsociety.co.uk, the top 100 charities raised £11.4 billion. You can see that Givenomics could easily match almost half of what the top 100 charities raise every year. Most importantly, the financial outcome would be spread out across a much larger number of organisations by empowering each person to choose their own causes.

On a behavioural level, millions of people would be used to giving in a way that is part of the fabric of their everyday lives and is just something that becomes normal and part of their buying behaviour. Looking at various initiatives that relate to giving, many have phrases that express the establishing of new giving norms – Givenomics does this on a vast scale.

Looking at the full opportunity, Givenomic schemes could easily match, if not exceed, the most popular fundraising events every year with a giving behaviour that is more proactive, does not rely on a guilt response and could even help us all to feel happier.

Connecting Businesses to Causes

All Businesses Become Part of a Powerful Force for Good

If all commercial organisations used a Givenomic model for their business, collectively they could become a real force for social impact that can be tracked, measured and reported on. This kind of reporting and tracking can easily extend from a local community to a regional, national and international level.

The perception of businesses and the support of people for their commercial success would be positively changed. Businesses that are successful should be celebrated and Givenomics provides a way of doing this that relates performance to social impact and would enable others to validate and publicise this information.

Local causes and local media, for example, would want to highlight organisations that have had considerable positive impact either to them directly or to the local area.

National media would be able to pick up the larger, national organisations in the same way. There would be a reason for us all to want businesses in our communities, in our regions, in our countries to be successful as they could be, helping the causes we support as their customers or employees.

Smaller Causes Benefit Too

One of the great things about the mass adoption of a Givenomic model is the level playing field it provides for the smaller causes who do not have the resources of larger ones to get the same level of support. I include schools in this because the supporter base there is naturally limited to the current parental audience, potentially some of their extended family and some local businesses.

The opportunity to highlight, share and celebrate some of these smaller organisations is inherent in the model and is a real strength and opportunity to foster deeper connectivity between these organisations, commercial companies and the people who support them.

As a trustee of what I would describe as a smaller cause, the opportunity to secure more funding from its supporter base is incredibly attractive and I know that this leads to additional positive impact on the community and the people East Herts YMCA serves. This story would be the same for many thousands of causes across the UK.

People Become Happier

Millions of people would be involved in making regular and tangible impact to the world around them. This level of penetration would mean that even if you weren't participating, someone you knew would be. Even a Givenomic scheme as it exists now, would give direct and tangible feedback and reward the giving behaviour with messaging designed to help people feel good about what they are doing.

On such a massive scale of deployment, the human psychology studies to date would suggest that millions of people could feel just that bit happier in general. That would be quite an outcome to consider. Why wouldn't anyone want that?

How to Achieve the Givenomic Vision

B2C Businesses Adopt Givenomics in Large Numbers

The possibility of all businesses adopting Givenomics may be too much of a stretch but once a critical mass has been reached, there will be a tipping point after which it will be a majority activity and it will become a social norm.

There are already many different loyalty schemes being implemented on a national, regional, local or even down to a single shop level that could leverage Givenomics as part of that loyalty mechanism.

Just looking at the number of businesses in the UK (4.5 million or so), it would need a significant number of the largest and B2C ones to adopt Givenomics as part of a primary business model and not a bolt on.

With the right environment, awareness and support, this is entirely possible.

B2B Businesses Adopt Givenomics in Large Numbers

While the mechanics of how Givenomics would work in the B2B environment are slightly different, the same basic principles apply, although consumer loyalty programmes would not be applicable in this case. As I outlined earlier, there is a great opportunity to engage customers and staff to maximise the success of many companies and therefore their Givenomic outcome.

Looking at the number of businesses in the UK, it would only take a few of the major trade bodies to endorse a Givenomic approach and help develop models that would work well for different types of B2B businesses to reach a tipping point.

Financial Companies can Adopt Givenomics on Large Scale

Just imagine if banks took a Givenomic approach to their business. When you consider the profits that many make, a small percentage given to the causes chosen by customers would create an incredible connectivity between customers, banks and causes. Banks have justifiably suffered a huge loss in confidence over the last decade and it is incumbent upon them to regain the trust of their customers and society in general. Givenomics would be a great part of this change.

The many transaction process companies could also be part of the growing number of companies engaging with a Givenomic model (eg. Visa, MasterCard, PayPal). Enabling a small giving element with each transaction would be easy to do if they had the strategic will to make it happen and the will to empower all their customers to choose their causes to support.

The billions of transactions made every year could have such a significant impact on people, their causes and thus a positive impact on the financial companies that enable it to happen.

Don't Wait,
Get Involved

So you made it to the end – well done. So what next? Make a commitment to contribute an even bigger, positive impact to communities you live in, companies you work in, causes that mean something to you and beyond. It will make you happier and you'll benefit others at the same time – it makes sense. Here are some suggestions to help you get started.

- Be proactive and choose to make a difference today. Don't wait to be asked by someone else. Think about what matters to you and focus your efforts to help in some way.

- If you already shop online for home or business, join www.TheGivingMachine.co.uk and start giving for free. There is a huge amount of money that can be diverted back into our communities – help make that happen.

- Encourage your company to consider how to include its customers and staff in a Givenomic model.

- If you are a business owner/leader and need help in considering how your organisation could benefit from a Givenomic approach, have some feedback to share, want to interview me or book me to speak to your team or company, get in touch.

- If you have ideas of your own, don't wait. Take the first steps to making them happen. Get in touch if you think I can help.

- Check www.Givenomics.com for other Givenomic schemes. If you find one, let me know and we can update the blog to spread the word.

- If you have any other feedback that you'd like to share – get in touch!

richard@givenomics.com

www.Givenomics.com

Twitter: @Givenomics @rjmorris67 @GivingMachineUK

About the Author

Richard has been a pioneer in both Silicon Valley and the UK, building the internet infrastructure and services we use as utilities today. Wanting to focus more on social impact, he co-founded and manages TheGivingMachine, a not-for-profit social enterprise that enables us all to shop and give for free to the causes of our choice. Enabling personalised, free giving as a behaviour choice is his passion and so far, over 500,000 free donations have been generated benefiting thousands of UK charities and schools via TheGivingMachine. Richard is also a trustee and vice chair of East Herts YMCA and lives in Bishop's Stortford with his wife Connie, two children (Alexandra and James), Max the dog and nine fish.

Lightning Source UK Ltd.
Milton Keynes UK
UKOW051043170113

204971UK00007B/78/P